Living with
grief and mourning

KING ALFRED'S COLLEGE
School of Health

Living with

Each book in this series deals with a medical or psychological condition. It contains background and medical information on causes and symptoms and explains treatment in some detail – both practical (drug treatments, surgery) and psychological (self-help, home care, social implications)

Series editors: John Riordan and Bob Whitmore

Living with
grief
and mourning

James Moorey

Manchester University Press

Manchester and New York

Distributed exclusively in the USA
and Canada by St. Martin's Press

Published by Manchester University Press
Oxford Road, Manchester M13 9NR, UK
and Room 400, 175 Fifth Avenue, New York, NY 10010, USA

Distributed exclusively in the USA and Canada
by St. Martin's Press, Inc.,
175 Fifth Avenue, New York, NY 10010, USA

British Library Cataloguing-in-Publication Data
A catalogue record for this book is available from the British Library

Library of Congress Cataloging-in-Publication Data
Moorey, James. 1954-
    Living with grief and mourning / James Moorey.
       p.   cm. — (Living with)
    Includes bibliographical references.
    ISBN 0-7190-3944-4. — ISBN 0-7190-3945-2 (pbk.)
    1. Grief. 2. Bereavement—Psychological aspects. 3. Loss
(Psychology) 4. Death—Psychological aspects.   I. Title.
II. Series.
BF575.G7M654   1995
155.9'37—dc20   94-40872
                        CIP

ISBN 0 7190 3944 4 *hardback*
ISBN 0 7190 3945 2 *paperback*

First published 1995

99 98 97 976 95   10 9 8 7 6 5 4 3 2 1

Typeset in New Century Schoolbook
by Koinonia, Manchester
Printed in Great Britain
by Bell & Bain Ltd, Glasgow

Contents

Acknowledgements

I would like to thank Debra Stackwood for her typing and Mark Fletcher for his generosity in a moment of crisis. I would also like to thank all those I have worked with in therapy and whose stories form the bulk of this book.

Preface

It is hoped that this book will be helpful to a wide range of readers, including professional and voluntary carers, those who have suffered bereavements, and families, friends and neighbours of the bereaved, who would like to offer them help and support.

Although loss and grief are unavoidable, the pain associated with grief can be understood, and to some extent at least, rendered more manageable.

The first two chapters contain most of the ideas that form the basis of the understanding of loss, grief and morning which underlie the rest of the book. These two chapters draw on insights from various disciplines which offer alternative perspectives on the subject, and taken together provide a wide-ranging understanding of the varied and complex human response to loss. Chapter 1 focuses on processes that operate for people everywhere regardless of background. Chapter 2 focuses on the way society and culture can mould, or shape, the experience of loss.

Chapters 3 and 4 contain descriptions of specific types of loss as they may occur throughout the various stages of the life cycle.

Chapters 5 to 9 focus on specific aspects of bereavement with an emphasis in each chapter on the practicalities of adjusting to loss, both in terms of the tasks facing the mourner, and how relatives, friends and neighbours can provide help and support. When reading this material it is important to bear in mind that the most significant factor in recovering from loss is the degree to which the bereaved person feels helped and supported by other people. Although at times other people can be a source of annoyance or disappointment, they can also be our greatest source of encouragement and hope.

Throughout this book experiences of those who have been bereaved are described. In each example the names and certain details have been changed in order to preserve anonymity.

James Moorey

1 Loss, grief and mourning

It is often said that the pain we feel when someone we love dies is the price we must pay for having loved them. Anyone who has gone through it will know that losing a loved person is one of the most painful experiences we can suffer. For many of us the loss of a loved person will be the most distressing experience of our life.

Losing a loved person can be compared to being physically injured. In fact many of those who have experienced it describe the death of a loved one as being like an amputation, like losing a limb. A major loss, like a physical injury, brings pain and distress in the short term, and often leaves a deep wound which can take a very long time to heal. 'Complications' can develop during recovery from a physical injury, wounds can reopen, and we can be left with permanent scars. As we shall see, each of these features of the process of recovery from a physical injury provide a helpful analogy for understanding grief and mourning.

The terms 'grief' and 'mourning' have been used in various ways, often interchangeably. I will use the word 'grief' to refer to the emotional response to loss; that is, what a person *feels*. And I will use the term 'mourning' to refer to the process of adjusting to, or recovering from, loss; the focus being on what a person *does*.

To understand why the death of a loved one provokes such intense pain and disruption we must consider exactly what it is that has been lost. We must understand what the loss means to the bereaved person; in other words the *significance* of the loss. In the first two sections of this chapter we will look at what it means to be attached to someone, and we will consider the formation of personal identity. In the third and fourth sections we will see how these factors shed light on the experience of grief and the process of mourning.

Attachment and loss

If you think back through your life you will probably be able to recall many losses. Some were doubtlessly more painful than others. Our personal losses may include friendships, possessions, opportunities, employment, ambitions, youth and many others. We can lose many things. We talk of 'losing face', 'losing interest', 'losing faith', 'losing our looks'; we even speak of 'losing ourselves' and 'losing our mind'. In the course of a lifetime it is inevitable that we will experience many losses, but fortunately most of these will be minor. Some losses we can dismiss as trivial, some may upset us for a few hours, or a few days; but some losses can hit us so hard that we feel we will never recover.

Losing a loved one is a comparatively rare event in an individual's life, but the experience is likely to be a traumatic one, perhaps the most traumatic experience of a person's life. The pain and distress resulting from such a major loss is likely to be severe, and recovery from the loss can take a long time. It is also important to note that there are very wide variations in the way people respond to loss. This is a point that will be emphasised throughout this book. But what is it that determines the way we respond to loss? In particular, what is it that determines the intensity of our response to loss? This is the same as asking: what is it that determines the significance of a loss?

These questions can be answered in a number of ways. We will look at two of the most important factors in this and the following section. This section will focus on the contribution of British psychiatrist and psychoanalyst, John Bowlby. Bowlby and his colleagues have developed what is known as Attachment Theory. This theory focuses on the 'making and breaking of affectional bonds'. On the basis of Attachment Theory it can be argued that it is the nature and quality of our attachments that exerts a primary influence on the intensity of our grief and our experience of loss. Hence, according to Bowlby, to understand why we react to loss in the way we do, we need to look at our attachments.

To 'attach' is to connect, fasten, tie or bind one thing to another. We can become attached to many things, objects as well as people. We can be attached to possessions, to our job, to a particular role we have in life, to an image we have of ourselves, to places, to money, and to many other things. When we form an attachment to someone, or something, we establish a tie or a bond with that person or thing. We are then connected, linked, or tied, in some way. Although the tie, the connection, is not physical, we are attached psychologically, or more specifically, emotionally.

The way we talk about relationships often implies a kind of tie, and it is this tie, this link or connection, that we refer to when we consider the formation of attachment. We talk of 'bonds' of affection, of being 'stuck' on someone, and of children being 'tied to mother's apron strings'. We talk of 'cutting' someone off, or 'breaking ties', 'severing links' and 'detaching' ourselves when relationships end. We also talk of how secure the tie or attachment is. A boat insecurely attached to a mooring may drift or be pulled away. Similarly the attachments in relationships can be strong or weak, secure or insecure. The nature of the attachment, how securely we are connected or tied, is revealed when the connection is threatened or severed, as it is by separation or by death.

If you are attached to someone it means you are strongly motivated to stay close to, or remain in contact with, that person. Bowlby uses the expression 'attachment behaviour' to refer to any behaviour that is aimed at attaining or maintaining closeness to a valued person. Attachment behaviour in some form continues throughout life, but is most evident in infancy.

At birth the infant must undergo his or her first separation. The foetus is attached to the mother by the umbilical cord. This tie has been vital for the survival of the embryo, but at birth the link must be severed. Here a literal physical connection is broken, but the connection with the mother (or someone else who can provide necessary care) is vital for survival. The tie that replaces the umbilical cord is just as necessary for the infant's survival. For most children growing up in Britain the primary attachment will be to the mother, who is usually the primary care-giver. Infants are clearly dependent on their mother for food, but this attachment provides more than just physical nourishment. This has been clearly demonstrated in animal research.

Attachment behaviour has been studied in the young of many species of birds, mammals and primates. In the 1930s ethologist Conrad Lorenz described the way in which ducklings and goslings instinctively follow their mother and manifest strong attachment despite the fact that the parent birds do not feed the young – the young feed themselves by catching insects. That attachments form for reasons other than securing supplies of food was also demonstrated by a series of experiments carried out in the 1950s and the 1960s by American psychologist Harry F. Harlow. Harlow took infant monkeys away from their mothers and gave them two substitute artificial monkey-dolls. One of the monkey-dolls was made of wire with a bottle attached from which the infant monkey could suckle. The second monkey-doll was made of spring rubber and cloth, hence was much softer than the wired monkey-doll, but it did not have a bottle for feeding. Infant monkeys showed strong attachment to the soft mother substitute, clinging to 'her' even when feeding from the milk attached to the wire monkey-doll. These experiments indicate the infant monkey's attempt to stay close, or remain attached, to its mother is not simply an attempt to ensure reliable sources of food. The infant monkey derives security from the physical presence of the mother over and above being supplied with food.

According to Bowlby, the biological function of attachment behaviour is essentially that of protection. Infants that stay close to a parent have more chance of survival than those inclined to wander off. Bowlby considers attachment behaviour to be as fundamental as feeding and sex, and just as necessary for the survival of the species. Of course we must be careful about applying results of animal experiments to humans, but essentially the same point – that attachment is motivated by more than need for nourishment – is true also of human infants. Essentially the infant develops attachment to a place of safety, a 'secure base', from which gradual explorations into the surroundings can occur. Typically, periods of clinging alternate with periods of exploration. The infant (for the sake of simplicity I will refer to the infant as 'he' in this section) gradually extends the distance at which he feels comfortable from the parent. (In this discussion I will assume the primary attachment is to the mother, as this will be the case for most infants in Britain.)

Even from the first weeks of life, the infant engages with his mother. By the end of the first year most infants will be able to realise that when an object passes out of its view, it still exists.

If you pass an object, say a bottle, behind a towel or behind your back, the very young infant will not follow it with his eyes. It's as if the object has ceased to exist for the child: 'out of sight, out of mind', as we say. However, by about the end of the first year the infant will follow the hidden object (or try to pull the towel away to see the hidden object), as if he knows the object still exists even though it cannot be seen. This is a very important step which the Swiss psychologist Jean Piaget called the development of 'object permanence' – the realisation that things continue to exist even when they cannot be seen. Some researchers have argued that 'person permanence' may develop earlier in the first year of life, and particularly in relation to the infant's mother. This capacity to understand that things or people continue to exist even when they are not seen or felt is the basic foundation on which the experience of loss, and hence grief, is built. Towards the end of the first year the infant will search for his mother when she is absent, and displays unmistakable attachment behaviour.

'Attachment behaviour' in infants is anything done by the infant to gain and regain closeness to the mother. Infants may cry, call, smile, cling and follow, all aimed at catching the mother's attention and keeping physically close. Attachment behaviour in human infants can be observed from about nine or ten weeks. The infant will smile when close to his mother, and cry if held by others, he will follow the mother with his eyes, cry when she disappears from view, crawl towards her, and cling to her, especially when alarmed or distressed for any reason. Attachment behaviours of this very obvious type continue until about the age of three when they begin to decline in frequency and intensity. However, attachment behaviour in some form persists throughout the life cycle. Bowlby sees the upheavals of adolescence as a critical time of transition, involving reduction of attachment to the family of origin and the formation of new attachments with others outside the family. A new 'secure base' has to be established, usually in the context of a sexual relationship. Attachment behaviour is particularly likely to re-emerge at times of stress, fatigue, illness, change, and most strikingly, at times of loss.

A situation which clearly reveals both the presence and the nature of an attachment bond is that of separation. During the 1950s the impact of separation on young children was studied by John Bowlby and his colleague James Robertson, a psychiatric social worker. A film made by Robertson in 1952, *A Two-Year-Old Goes to Hospital*, vividly portrays the impact of separation on an infant. It appears that when children between about twelve months and three years are separated from their mother a typical sequence of responses can often be observed. The separation is usually followed by a period of 'protest'. In this phase the infant is restless, cries and searches for his mother. The infant appears anxious, fearful, and insecure. As the infant's goal of re-establishing closeness to the mother is frustrated, he will often become very angry. Ultimately this anger is felt towards the mother who is seen as the prime source of the frustration. In effect the infant is trying to force his mother to respond, by gaining her attention, and also to punish her to make sure she doesn't leave him in the same way again. As well as being angry the infant resists being comforted by others. The infant is clearly uncomfortable with the separation and is trying to re-establish closeness by attachment behaviour that has previously been successful in gaining the mother's attention.

This initial response may last a week or so but if the separation continues the 'protest' will usually be followed by a period of 'despair', during which the child will seem inconsolable, as if he has given up trying to regain closeness with his mother. The infant withdraws and quietens but the despair is evident in continuing bouts of sobbing, and often hostile reactions to anyone who offers comfort.

If the separation continues this period will often be followed by a period of 'detachment' in which the infant will seem indifferent to the presence or absence of his mother. If the mother returns at this point the child will continue to display detachment (although observers have noted this detachment will not be shown to the father if he also returns). The sequence – protest, despair, detachment – looks as if the child has tried to regain the closeness it had with mother through the well-practised strategies of attachment behaviour, but when this fails the child resigns himself to the loss and finally detaches. The end result is a severing of the bonds, (that is de-attachment), which can take considerable time to re-establish.

An infant's attachment behaviour has as its goal the attainment and preservation of a physically close connection with his mother. Attachment behaviours – crying, calling, searching, following – are intensified if the mother cannot be seen, or the separation becomes prolonged, as demonstrated by Robertson's film. It is important to recognise that these behaviours are extremely valuable. An infant's life depends on staying close to his mother. Human infants, and young animals, will try to stick close to their mother as if it were a matter of life or death, as in many cases it will be. It is through this vital attachment that the infant gains nourishment, protection, care and security. It is not surprising that separation and the threatened loss of this secure base provokes such an intense response, which is aimed at re-establishing contact with the source of security and protection.

John Bowlby has argued that attachment behaviour follows a largely instinctive pattern, that the tendency to form and try to preserve close attachments is something all humans inherit as part of their biological make-up. Attachment behaviour is based on the assumption that loss is recoverable, that the separation will be temporary. This is clearly seen in the way that the various behaviours provoked by separation are aimed at retrieving what has been lost. The intensity of the calling, crying, and searching, needs to be strong enough to motivate the searcher and summon the care-giver. These behaviours show that the bond, the attachment, is still intact. It is only when these behaviours fail to recover the loss, when the separation seems permanent, that the response changes and finally the bond can be broken as the infant 'detaches'.

The child's responses of anxiety and anger ('protest'), and sadness and depression ('despair'), may seem perfectly understandable and natural under the circumstances, but the third phase of 'detachment' is not so easily understood. It is useful to look in more detail at what is occurring when the infant 'detaches'. Bowlby has suggested the best way of understanding this is in terms of 'psychological defences'.

In order to understand what defences are it is helpful to begin by thinking about our normal everyday experience, what we are aware of from moment to moment. One of the major characteristics of our ordinary experience is that it is highly selective. Try to imagine what it would be like to be fully aware of everything that is happening around you, and to you. Imagine being aware of all your sensations. Notice for a moment the sensation in your hands, your arms, your back, your legs and feet. Notice the sensations in your mouth, on your face and scalp. Notice the movement of your eyes, and of your breathing. Notice the various sights and sounds of your surroundings. Try to imagine, at the same time, being fully aware of everything that has happened to you in the past, including everything you have seen and heard, felt and thought. It is of course impossible to imagine such a situation: we can only cope with a very narrow range of experiences at any one time. Mercifully our nervous system has evolved very effective methods for excluding vast amounts of information from our awareness. Some of this information could be transformed into conscious experience quite easily – for example, by remembering what happened yesterday. Other things are much harder, perhaps even impossible, to be aware of. Evolution has shaped our nervous system to respond primarily to information vital for our survival. Much information not immediately required for the serious business of staying alive is effectively excluded from our awareness. Hence our moment by moment awareness is a product of careful selection and exclusion of information about both the environment and our inner world. Without these restrictions on what we experience we would be overwhelmed.

Now there are very many ways in which this selection and exclusion of information can occur. For our purposes we need to look at a group of processes that exclude from awareness information of a very special type. These processes are termed 'psychological defences'. Under certain conditions these defences can actively prevent us from experiencing specific aspects of our environment, and most significantly, particular aspects of ourselves. Our defences are themselves operating largely outside of our awareness, that is, we are not aware that we are actively preventing ourselves from having particular experiences. As the name implies 'defences' operate to protect us, to shield us from intense anxiety or psychological pain. Often what is being excluded from our awareness, what we are preventing ourselves from experiencing, is associated with some kind of conflict. Consider an example. A male employee is given severe criticism for poor work performance by an exacting employer. The employee feels hurt, embarrassed and angry. As he is also frightened of his boss he takes the criticism without comment. His conflict is clear: he would like to retaliate and vent his anger on his boss, but this impulse conflicts with his fear that he may lose his job. After work our employee returns home. That evening he explodes in anger at his wife because the house is untidy. He is trying to deal with the conflict at work by venting his anger at home. He reduces his own humiliation by humiliating his wife. He remains defensively unaware of what he has done and insists his anger is justified. (This is such a common way of managing difficult feelings – displacing them from one situation onto another – that our employee may have been dimly aware of what he was doing. However, many defences are very much more subtle, and occur completely outside of our awareness.)

To return to the infant's response to prolonged separation from his mother we can note a very pronounced conflict. The infant experiences intense anxiety over his mother's absence, and a desperate longing for her return. But the infant also experiences intense anger that this need has been frustrated by her continued absence. The same person – the mother – is the focus of very intense and conflicting feelings. The infant desperately wants to feel comforted, and feel secure, but also wants to attack the source of frustration. The mother is the focus of both love and hate. The conflict is naturally very distressing for the infant. So how can a young child, faced with such turmoil, cope with these painful feelings?

We have noted that much of what occurs during the phases of 'protest' and 'despair' is a desperate attempt to regain closeness to the mother. The child is seeking to re-establish the sense of safety and security associated with being physically close to his mother. The pain of separation is the vital prompt to search for the lost person, who represents security, care, and protection. Without the suffering the child's search would be less intense, less persistent, and in many cases less effective. But when the loss is not recovered, when the mother is not found or does not return, the attachment behaviour, demonstrated during the 'protest' and 'despair' phases ceases to be of value. The child shuts down, or turns off, the attachment behaviours, defensively excluding from his awareness anything which might continue to provoke them. In other words he 'detaches'.

It is important to note that although the child initially tries to regain closeness with the mother, if this is unsuccessful he will act in a self-protecting way to reduce the pain and suffering, by emotional detachment. In relation to the mother the 'detached' child is 'cut off': he will appear to be without feeling for her. The child is 'cut off' from his mother and from his pain. The connection has been severed, or rather a concerted attempt has been made to sever the connection, in order to deal with the emotional pain of loss. Detachment is defensive or self-protective, and is usually developed in relation to one person, the mother, who has persistently failed to respond to the child's efforts to re-establish closeness to her. This detachment does not usually extend to other people or prevent the formation of new attachments, or indeed the re-establishing of the former level of attachment to the mother. In fact observers have noted that after the mother has returned there will often be a period where she will be ignored by the child, but after a while the child will become very clinging, or 'anxiously attached' to her. Hence the psychological defence of 'detachment' can be regarded as helpful so long as it does not extend to others or become permanent. 'Detachment' makes sense when we see it as a form of self-protection, as a way of reducing the pain of loss.

This description provides an outline of a healthy infant's response to separation. But not all infants exhibit this pattern of behaviour. American psychologist Mary Ainsworth and her colleagues have identified four major patterns of attachment that children can form with their mother or primary care-giver. 'Secure' attachment is one pattern that can be reliably identified. With this type of relationship the infant experiences his mother as a reliable, responsive, and helpful presence. This assurance enables the child to use closeness to his mother as a secure base from which to explore his surroundings with confidence. The child is able to act with the assurance that if he gets into difficulty his mother will respond reliably and effectively.

A second pattern identified by Ainsworth is that of 'resistant' attachment. With this pattern the infant lacks the confidence and assurance of the 'secure' attachment. The child is unsure about the response of the mother. The uncertainty appears to develop because the mother has been persistently erratic in providing reliable and effective responses to the child's attachment behaviour. The child becomes cautious, unwilling to explore, anxious and clinging, and particularly prone to react with intense anxiety when separated from his mother.

The third pattern described by Ainsworth is that of 'avoidant' attachment. In this pattern the child not merely lacks confidence and assurance that his attachment behaviour will be reliably responded to but rather expects to be rejected. In extreme cases the infant will attempt to survive without forming attachments, and try to become emotionally self-sufficient.

The fourth pattern is that of 'disorganised' attachment. There are relatively few infants who display this pattern, but it includes a range of unpredictable and apparently disorientated behaviours, such as inhibited and repetitive activities when the infant is reunited with his mother after separation.

Despite the fact that it is extremely difficult to obtain reliable research data in this area, it appears that once established these attachment patterns persist, and influence the formation of intimate relationships in adult life. We will return to consider some of the consequences of insecure attached in chapter 8.

In the early 1960s John Bowlby drew attention to the similarities between an infant's response to separation and the way adults respond to the death of a loved person. The continued study of attachment in infancy and in adult life has shed light on some crucial areas of grief and mourning. First, it has been noted that many features of grief and mourning can be understood as serving a similar purpose to the child's response to separation; that is, initially, as attempts to recover the loss, followed by efforts to adjust or adapt to the irreversibility of the loss. Second, childhood patterns of attachment, and experience of separation and loss, can have a profound influence on the way adult relationships are formed and maintained, and how an adult responds to loss. The first of these points will be elaborated in the rest of this chapter, and we will consider the second point in chapter 8.

Loss and personal identity

Attachment Theory is an important contribution to our understanding of responses to loss. But while Bowlby has emphasised the biological, or instinctive, features of grief and mourning, other researchers have focused more on the psychological and social dimensions. In this section we will review some of the work that has been done on the development and maintenance of an individual's sense of personal identity, or sense of self. In the context of this work the loss of a loved person can be seen as a threat to the self, and certain aspects of grief and mourning can be understood in terms of a person's response to that threat.

The study of personal identity, of a person's sense of self, is a complex and controversial subject. At the risk of over-simplification we will restrict our attention to some basic points that are particularly relevant to a person's response to loss. 'Identity' has various meanings but we will focus on identity as being our sense of who or what we are. Our identity is all of those things that distinguish us from others, or that would enable us to be recognised. Our identity comprises a mixture of unique attributes – which differentiate us from others – and characteristics we share with others. If we had to describe ourselves – or to put this another way, if we had to identify ourselves – we could list a great many things. We may think of various 'identities', such as national, racial, gender, and sexual identities. We may consider our appearance and physical attributes, including features such as age, height, weight, colour of hair and eyes, clothing, etc. We may describe ourselves in terms of a central relationship or set of relationships. We may be a husband or wife, a mother of four, an eldest son, a younger brother, a big sister, a grandfather of six. We may identify ourselves in terms of our employment: as a schoolteacher, a bus driver, a company director, a clerk, a mechanic, a hairdresser. We may see ourselves as a complex mix of personal attributes, some of which we like and some we dislike. We may think of attributes such as generosity, impatience, humour, inefficiency, kindness, laziness, intelligence, dependency, secrecy, envy, friendliness, and of course many others.

Our personal identity, who or what we consider ourselves to be, clearly involves a great many things. Our sense of personal identity, our sense of self, embraces all of those things we call 'me', including our various roles, attributes and characteristics. But to get deeper into this notion of identity, or sense of self, we can reflect on how we feel about ourselves. We may feel happy or depressed with who or what we are (or rather who or what we think we are). We may be trying actively to change. We may dislike aspects of ourselves, or feel guilt about something we have done, or ashamed of what we feel, or anger at how we have been treated. We may be content or we may be resentful. We may feel we are in the wrong job, or in the wrong relationship, or even feel we are the wrong sex. Our sense of identity is clearly very much more than can be indicated by a list of roles of personal characteristics. Our sense of identity, our sense of self, is rooted in our emotions.

If we reflect further on our sense of personal identity we may notice four fundamental assumptions. First, the self persists through time. Second, the self is bounded, or contained within a body, and separate from other selves. Third, the self can initiate and control its own activities; 'I' can decide, choose, will and act independently of other selves. And fourth, the self is individual, each person is just one self. The impact of loss can be clarified by considering these assumptions in more detail.

An important implication of the word 'identity' is the notion of persistence through time. If we are to be able to identify anything, regardless of what it is, there must be at least some consistent features that allow us to recognise that something seen at one point in time is the same as that seen at another. The aspects of identity listed in the above paragraphs cover relatively consistent characteristics of a person; their appearance, their roles and their personality. What we take to be our personal identity, or sense of self, what we call 'me', persists through time, both the past as remembered and the future as imagined. Whenever we think about what we will do in the future, we predict that we will be much the same as we are today. We assume our identity is relatively fixed. However, when we think of how we were ten, twenty, or thirty years ago, we may consider that we have undergone dramatic changes. And yet we believe we are the same person, although it may be very difficult to say in what way we are the same. It is as if through all the changes there is some essence of the self, some essence of 'me', that continues. Persistence through time is clearly of fundamental importance in our sense of personal identity.

Our second assumption is that the self has control over its own activity. Underlying our sense of responsibility and personal accountability is the idea that people can choose how to behave. The self is considered to be a centre of choice, able to decide and intend, and able to carry out what it wills. For example, I can choose whether to continue writing or to go for a walk; I can choose what to think about and what to ignore; some would argue I can even chose my moods. Some degree of control and mastery is fundamental to our sense of self. Indeed some would argue we *are* our choices. But when we look through our list of the various aspects of personal identity, it is obvious that many of the characteristics listed are not themselves the result of choice. Also we may note that within the self, or within our own minds, we can observe that some things seem to follow our intentions and others simply seem to happen to us. I might decide to think about a problem that I want to find a solution to: this appears to be a deliberate conscious choice. At other times I may find thoughts entering my mind unbidden, perhaps so persistently that my sleep is disturbed. Within this 'private self' it's as if there are divisions between aspects that I can control and aspects that have a life of their own, that I am powerless to influence.

Our third assumption is that each person is just one self. Looking at our list of characteristics of personal identity we may notice that some aspects of our identity are very private, to do with our personal 'inner world', while other aspects are more to do with how we are with others. A rough distinction is often made between our private, or 'personal self', and our public or 'social self'. (If we examine this distinction too closely it soon breaks down, but it is useful as a first approximation.) How we are when we are alone will differ in important respects from how we are with others. When we reflect on this we may feel that our private self is perhaps more genuinely who we are than our social self. We may feel that to some extent our social self is assumed or 'put on', in order to ensure that we get on with others reasonably well.

When we think about this 'private self', we can notice some very curious features. One is our capacity for self-reflection, or self-consciousness. The self can examine itself, we can investigate our own 'inner world'. We can be aware of what is happening within the self ('inside') as well as what is happening beyond the self ('outside'). I can be aware of my private thoughts, feelings, fantasies and memories. I can 'see' myself becoming anxious, or angry or sad; I can observe myself making plans, wasting time or worrying. It's almost as if the self can divide into a part that observes and a part that is being observed.

Despite the consistency and stability mentioned in the previous paragraph, we may experience episodes of uncharacteristic behaviour. If we act in a way that is inconsistent with how we imagine ourselves to be we may say 'I wasn't myself', or, 'I don't know what came over me'. Although overall we may have a sense of self that is consistent and coherent, our experience of ourself varies. Sometimes we are angry, sometimes we are sad; we may feel happy on one day and depressed the next. Sometimes we seem to cope well, at other times poorly. It's as if we are many selves that surface, or come into play, at different times. We seem to have many identities, and many selves that are associated with various roles and various feelings and perceptions. At times people experience themselves as being very different from who or what they thought they were, especially in unusual situations. 'I didn't know I had it in me', can mean 'I acted very differently to how I would have predicted'. It seems as if the 'I', or what is experienced as 'me', can switch from one self to another. When we talk of 'not being myself today', this suggests that we have (or are) what could be termed a dominant self or dominant 'I', but that other selves can be experienced as 'I'. It's as if the observing 'I' can relocate and experience the world from the perspective of another self. If this is how the private self appears, this is even more the case with the social self. We play many roles and can be quite different people in one situation compared to another. Rather than talking about a private and a social self, we may more appropriately talk about two collections of selves: 'private selves' and 'social selves'. Somehow all this variation is held together and a coherent identity seems to persist through it all, but the assumption that each person is, or has, just one unified self is certainly open to question. However, if we go on to ask what is it that does the observing and why some aspects of the self are apparently under voluntary control and others are not, we shall enter a swamp of controversy that has vexed philosophers and psychologists for centuries. For our purposes we can gratefully ignore these problems.

Our fourth assumption is that the self is separate from other selves, and bounded by a body. But again this common assumption may not be entirely correct. Often it is easy to see how two people who are closely attached have come to resemble one another. They take on aspects of each other's personality. It's as if a close bond with another human being brings us so close that psychologically we 'overlap'. This suggests people can come to resemble each other by imitation, but imitation is, psychologically speaking, a relatively superficial process. Close attachment often involves elements of 'identification', which is a process whereby people do not merely act like one another, they actually become like each other. The boundary between people who love each other is not clear cut. What after all does it mean to be 'close' to someone? How 'close' is 'close'? The closest we can be is when there is no distance at all between us and the other person. Then we would be indistinguishable, we would be the same person, we would have the same identity. The continuum between being totally identified with another and 'drifting apart' allows many degrees of 'closeness' or 'attachedness'. Attachment behaviour seeks closeness – physical and emotional – and although there are degrees of closeness, the boundaries between people, between selves, seem to be permeable.

This brings us to the main point of this section. Although we may describe or identify ourselves in many different ways, the various attributes, roles, behaviours, thoughts and feelings that we see as comprising who or what we are, are to a very large extent the product of relationships. Our identity is formed in relation to others, and those aspects of identity which seem more uniquely personal (what we call 'me') are to a very significant extent a reflection of important relationships. The self is formed through our interaction with other people, and will reflect both past and current relationships.

It's as if the important relationships in our life, or rather aspects of those relationships, are taken into ourselves, and become incorporated into, or absorbed into, what we call 'me'. It's as if we carry certain features of important relationships around inside ourselves. In particular it is the way we have been treated by people who have been significant to us that gets built into our sense of personal identity, our sense of self. There are a number of ways that we can take other people into ourselves, but we can use the term 'internalisation' to refer to these processes in general, meaning simply that something outside the self is taken inside. This process of 'internalisation' has a crucial influence on emotional development, self-esteem and intimate relationships.

'Internalisation' plays a part in the formation of our two sets of selves. The apparently more private 'I' is no less a product of relationships than any social role we choose to adopt. So it is important to note that all aspects of the self, everything we call 'me', have been constructed largely from our experience of significant relationships. This is as true of the private self – including the capacity for self-reflection – as it is for the social self. So that while the self may appear to be separate, distinct, and bounded (within one's own body), the boundary is in fact rather blurred, or, as noted earlier, is permeable. Both aspects of personal identity – private and social – may undergo change in the course of a person's life, primarily as a result of the influence of significant relationships. It is in and through relationships that we continue the work of clarifying and confirming our sense of who we are, our identity. We could even say that we build our world, and even our sense of reality, through these relationships.

We have noted that the self is assumed to have a consistent history, the ability to choose and exert control, and is believed to be individual and separate from other selves. But, as we have seen, these assumptions are perhaps not as straightforward as they initially appear. Loss of a significant relationship dramatically undermines all four assumptions. Hence a significant loss can be seen as an assault on the self. Because what is internal and what is external is somewhat blurred, an external loss is experienced, in part, as also being an internal loss. Because to some extent we are identified with the people we are close to, their death is felt to be, at least in part, our own death. In turn our sense of continuity, consistency and predictability, crucial to our sense of self, is undermined. Anticipating events accurately is essential to our feelings of well-being and our sense of self. Loss propels us into a radically unpredictable situation. Unpredictability is potentially dangerous, hence loss provokes anxiety. The loss of a significant relationship disrupts the ongoing process of self-construction and maintenance. At the same time our sense of control, or mastery, is challenged by the loss which we were powerless to prevent; and the disruptive power of our grief can be felt as uncontrollable and overpowering. Further, because such intense grief is usually an infrequent occurrence, new aspects of the self, or selves, may be experienced. We may feel 'beside ourselves with grief', disorientated and unlike our familiar self.

It would follow from the claim that an external loss is at the same time an internal loss that in order to recover from the injury of loss the bereaved person must rebuild their inner world, in particular their sense of self, or sense of identity.

Loss of a significant relationship leads to a crisis in the self: both its private and its social aspects must be rebuilt or reconstructed. As psychoanalyst Melanie Klein noted, the bereaved person must 'rebuild with anguish the inner world which is felt to be in danger of deteriorating and collapsing'. But what exactly is involved in this rebuilding? Various accounts have been offered, and we need not concern ourselves with the details, but generally there are two essential features. First, relocating the person who has died; and second, redefining the self. We will consider these two features in detail in the last two sections of this chapter.

The main point of these remarks on self-identity is to emphasise how profoundly we are changed by closeness to another person. From this we can see that the loss of a loved person – someone to whom we were very close – is in some sense a loss of identity; in some sense it is a loss of self. Physical pain signals danger, alerting us to a threat to our physical integrity, warning us of our vulnerability. The pain of grief similarly signals danger, an assault on the integrity of the self – a threat to our identity. Many of the experiences associated with grief and mourning can be seen as adaptive responses to this assault. The process of mourning involves striving to rebuild a sense of identity in the light of a significant loss. A major loss changes who, or what, we thought we were. David's wife in an instant becomes David's widow, a mother is suddenly childless, a child is suddenly fatherless. After years of companionship one finds oneself alone and 'single'. The bereaved person may have to learn new skills, and take on new roles: caring for children, domestic chores, perhaps finding, or giving up, employment. Loss can turn our world upside-down. And the clock cannot be turned back. No wonder such losses are often described as being the psychological equivalent of an amputation: 'I feel like my insides have been torn out', 'I feel I've lost a limb', 'I feel so cut up', 'part of me died with him', 'I feel completely empty'. With the loss of a loved person we lose something of ourselves.

Common features of grief

We have considered Attachment Theory and the formation of identity to help us understand why individuals respond to loss in the way they do. In this section we will look at common features of grief and mourning and see how these are made more comprehensible in the light of this information.

People respond to bereavement in many different ways. The loss will seem to permeate every aspect of the mourner's life, and every corner of their experience. In this section we will consider common features of grief, the feelings and associated thoughts and behaviours. Some of these features may appear disturbing or bizarre, but they are all very common, and can be considered essentially healthy responses to loss.

Feelings

Sadness is, of course, an expected response to loss. Sadness, even depression, is expected and in a sense 'respectable'. There are many other feelings which commonly occur as a result of bereavement, but which are not expected and, in a sense, not 'respectable'. These feelings will often be a cause of shame and guilt, and will often therefore be hidden.

Anxiety is frequently felt in relation to how the survivor will cope without the deceased. There may be dependents that need caring for and increased financial burdens, and other challenges that the survivor may fear they will not be able to meet. Another aspect of anxiety in bereavement is the increased awareness of one's own inevitable death, which may often be brought into focus after a major loss. Physical sensations typical of anxiety include breathlessness, tightness in the chest and throat, aching or weak muscles, dizziness, increased heart rate, perspiration, dry mouth, and a tendency to startle at sudden noise. These sensations may be accompanied by feelings of apprehension or even panic. These feelings can often be paralysing during the initial period of acute grief, but diminish as the survivor finds ways of coping without the deceased. Here we can note the connection with Bowlby's work on separation in infancy. For an infant to be left alone is a potentially dangerous state of affairs. Anxiety is therefore a natural and appropriate response to the threatening situation. Part of the fear is also related to the way a significant loss can undermine our sense of self. In fact it has often been noted how close the feeling of grief is to fear.

Anger is a common response to loss which can be particularly confusing and distressing for the bereaved person. Anger may be felt towards hospitals or others involved for not doing enough, or acting quickly enough, to prevent the loss. Anger may also be felt towards the survivor themselves for similar reasons. Perhaps even more disturbing is when anger is felt towards the deceased. Such anger is common, particularly where the bereaved person is left with increased responsibilities. Those who have been bereaved through suicide also often experience their loss as a personal rejection, and this can leave them feeling bitter and angry. Referring once again to Bowlby's work on attachment, it may be noted that the anger often associated with adult grief is comparable to the 'protest' of infants when separated from their mother. The function of the hostility is essentially to recover the person who is lost, and ensure they do not leave again. Underlying the anger is, of course, the pain of loss, the intensity of which is often a testimony to the strength of the attachment.

Another common response that may be very difficult to acknowledge is of feeling relieved that the person has died. This may be related to having watched the deceased suffer from a long illness or disability, and hence requiring a lot of care and attention which may have been a considerable strain on family and carers. Or there may have been long-standing difficulties or conflicts that have led the survivor to wish they were free of the person. Their subsequent death can then inspire relief. This may seem a perfectly understandable reaction, but it can lead the bereaved person to experience profound guilt. Guilt may also be felt if there is self-blame about the care that was provided or the response towards the deceased before they died.

Feeling lonely, pining, or yearning for the deceased are again very common feelings that diminish as the bereaved person gradually rebuilds their life without the deceased. Numbness, or absence of feeling, is also often experienced, particularly early on in the bereavement when the state of shock seems to inhibit feelings of any sort.

While it is true that most people suffering a major loss will experience such feelings as sadness, depression, despair, anxiety, anger, and other distressing emotions, this is by no means always the case. Recent research suggests that between a quarter and two-thirds of widows and widowers are not greatly distressed by their loss.

Thoughts

Often the initial response to loss is to think that it cannot possibly be true: 'This can't be happening to me, there must be some mistake', 'I keep thinking I will wake up and it will all have been a bad dream'. Such thoughts are very common. But as the truth sinks in many bereaved people will be beset by desperate questions such as: 'How could this happen?', and, 'Why me?' Critical thoughts will be common when there is the possibility that something could have been done to prevent the death (a more rapid response from the emergency services for example). But criticisms and blame, of self and others, is by no means restricted to these situations. Thinking that the loss may be a punishment, or thinking that the death must have some special purpose are very common thoughts. Thinking over the circumstances of the death, being preoccupied with the details, appears to be a way of trying to come to terms with what has happened.

As mentioned in the section on feelings, anxiety, sadness and depression are common responses to loss. These feelings will often be accompanied by thoughts which involve doubting one's ability to cope without the deceased and seeing no hope for the future: 'I can't accept it', 'I will never get over it', 'My life is finished', 'I will never meet anyone like him/her again'. In situations where the bereaved person had been very dependent on the deceased, the survivor's thoughts may become obsessed with the idea that it will be impossible for them to continue without them. This may lead to thoughts of ending their own life. Such thoughts are not uncommon after a major loss.

Many bereaved people experience the presence of the deceased person in the home or in particular rooms. For some this can be a source of comfort. But for others it can be very disturbing and cause them to avoid certain rooms or places where the presence is felt. Visual or verbal hallucinations of the deceased are also very common and once again people react to these experiences very differently; some are comforted and some are frightened. Some people see or hear the deceased very vividly, as if they were actually there with them. Others describe a much more fleeting, momentary image or voice. Holding conversations with the deceased, sometimes hearing replies as if the deceased person was actually in the room speaking to them, may continue for many months after the loss.

Dreams of the deceased, which again can be comforting, frightening or upsetting, frequently occur. Dreaming that there has been a mistake and that the person has not really died are common themes. Dreams about the deceased can be so vivid that on waking the dreamer may be startled and experience deep regret that, after all, they were just dreaming. Being preoccupied with the circumstances of the loss, imagining how it could have been different, or imagining receiving a phone call to say the person did not die, are all ways in which the reality of the loss may be resisted. In imagination the survivor may bargain with God to try to get the deceased back, if only for a short time. We can understand these experiences as an attempt to hold on to what is lost, an attempt to maintain the idea that the separation is not permanent, that the loss is recoverable. As we have noted, this idea – that the loss is recoverable – is the underlying assumption of the various forms of attachment behaviour that occur after separation. These attempts to deny the permanence of loss can be extremely persistent, continuing for months, perhaps even for years.

Behaviour

Often the bereaved person will want to withdraw from activities and from other people. It may be stressful to be with others because the bereaved person feels under pressure to respond in particular ways or because they feel their presence will put other people under pressure. This withdrawal can be very out of character – someone who previously enjoyed an active social life with many interests can become withdrawn and uncommunicative. But it may also happen that the bereaved person becomes very active, perhaps going out frequently, taking on new responsibilities, engaging in new activities. Both withdrawal and increased activity are common changes in behaviour following bereavement. Usually these changes are temporary and reflect differing ways of adjusting to loss. Withdrawal allows time for processing what has happened without having to give attention to other responsibilities. This response can be compared to Bowlby's description of the 'despair' phase which follows 'protest' after separation. Increased activity can also be helpful as a way of filtering what has occurred; that is, loss is allowed to 'sink in' over time, as a way of preventing being overwhelmed by what has happened.

Changes in sleep patterns and appetite are also frequently experienced after loss. Again individual differences are important: some people increase their sleep or food intake, others find it difficult to sleep or eat. Often it is the case that where the bereaved person has lost a spouse the loss may be particularly intensely felt at night or at mealtimes. The loss of a familiar presence at night and the loss of someone who prepared food, or for whom food was prepared, brings the reality of the loss home.

The bereaved person may try to avoid certain places, objects or situations that remind them of the dead person. For example, they may refuse to look at photographs, or listen to certain pieces of music. After the loss of a partner the survivor may avoid sleeping in the same bed, or bedroom. One widower in his sixties slept on the settee in his living room for a year following the death of his wife. He described a very gradual process of getting used to going into the bedroom for longer periods and finally being able to sleep in the bed on his own: 'Bit by bit I got used to her not being there. I never thought I would, but slowly being on my own came to feel normal.' Some bereaved people respond by trying to get rid of all reminders of the deceased, as if attempting to avoid anything that may confront them with their loss. Other bereaved people do the opposite: keeping things exactly as the deceased left them, as if waiting for them to return; or perhaps treating the deceased's room or belongings as a 'shrine'.

The process of mourning

We have likened a significant loss to receiving an injury. This injury naturally provokes pain and distress. Mourning can be understood as a process of recovery from the injury of loss. To describe mourning as a process suggests there are a number of elements contributing to a movement towards a particular goal. Recovering from a physical injury involves repair and recovery of function. Similarly, after a major loss the goal of recovery would involve re-establishing previous levels of functioning and moving on with life. Mourning is the process of adapting to loss. The process of mourning is necessary if we are to come to terms with loss. This process can be described in various ways, and over the last thirty years a number of prominent researchers have offered alternative descriptions. In this section we will consider two of the most influential accounts, the first describing the process in terms of 'Phases', the second in terms of 'Tasks'.

Phases of Mourning

John Bowlby has described the process of mourning in terms of four 'Phases'. In 1961 Bowlby published his first account of these phases and drew attention to the similarities between these and the infant's response to separation, which we have considered above. Since that early work there have been a number of modifications outlined in different publications, by both Bowlby and his colleague Colin Murray-Parkes. Here is a brief outline of the Four Phases of Mourning as they have been elaborated in Bowlby's later work:

Phase One: Numbness. A period of shock and numbness often occurs immediately after a loss. The numbness can be regarded as protective: allowing the truth to sink in slowly assists the person to cope with the pain. It's as if the bereaved person has administered an anaesthetic to themselves. In this way the mourner keeps the pain at bay temporarily in order that they are not overwhelmed by it.

Phase Two: Yearning. In this phase the reality of the loss is acknowledged, leading to a desperate longing for the deceased. The mourner may actively search for the dead person, going from room to room, hoping and expecting to see the familiar face of the person they have lost. They may scan the faces of people they pass on the street and think they have seen their loved one in the distance or in a crowd. The mourner may hear the voice of the deceased, and perhaps even see them. They may call out, begging them not to leave, or pleading with them to return. This searching may even lead the mourner to try to contact the dead person, perhaps through mediums or spiritualists. The bereaved person may go over the circumstances of the loss in minute detail, as if desperately searching for a way out, trying to discover that a mistake has been made, that the loss is not real. The desperation of the search is often fuelled by intense anxiety about what will happen if the loved person really has gone. Anger is likely to be felt towards anyone who confirms that the loss is real. Friends, hospital staff, God, and even the deceased, often become targets of the mourner's anger. Bowlby considers these feelings and behaviours to have a very precise goal: to recover what has been lost, to be reunited with the deceased. This phase of mourning is comparable to the 'protest' phase of separation, as described above.

Phase Three: Disorganisation. As it becomes clear that the efforts to recover the lost person are failing, the realisation that the loss is irreversible sinks in. The bereaved person may feel devastated and disorientated. The impact of the loss may provoke deep sadness and withdrawal into a state of apathy and helplessness. For some this may lead to depression and despair. The mourner may feel there is no point to their life. Their sense of who they are and their place in the world may be completely overturned. The bereaved person may feel they are 'falling apart', and that they will never be able to pick up the pieces. Again we may note the similarities between this phase of mourning and the phase of 'despair' following separation, described above.

Phase Four: Reorganisation. The process of rebuilding a life shattered by a major loss often involves developing new skills and taking on new roles. Learning to live without the deceased can be a lengthy process that rarely progresses smoothly, without setbacks. In the case of the loss of a close attachment Bowlby sees an essential part of the reorganisation phase as being the rebuilding of a new 'secure base'; a new sense of safety from which the mourner can once again go out into the world and engage with the pressures and demands of everyday life. Certain features of this phase of mourning are similar to the 'detachment' phase following separation which was described above.

Some have argued that a weakness of this account is that it implies that the person moves rather passively through a process that happens *to* them. It is probably more accurate to see mourning as something a person *does*. The process of mourning has certain objectives, it has a particular function. This is suggested by a frequently quoted remark of Sigmund Freud: 'Mourning has a quite precise psychical task to perform: its function is to detach the survivor's memories and hopes from the dead.' The overall task of mourning is to break the attachment, or the bond, that existed between the mourner and the deceased, and to re-establish it in a different form. This involves activity on the part of the mourner; the mourner has to do something, hence the use of the expression 'grief work'. From this perspective the process of mourning can be seen as involving certain specific tasks.

Tasks of Mourning

American psychologist William Worden has suggested that mourning can be understood as a process involving four essential tasks. There are specific activities that need to be done if the process is to be satisfactorily completed. The outline given here is a summary of the Four Tasks of Mourning as presented by Worden in the second edition of his book *Grief Counselling and Grief Therapy* (1991):

Task One: To Accept the Reality of the Loss. Many bereaved people initially react to their loss with disbelief. 'This cannot be true, there must be a mistake' is a very common reaction to loss. Later, the loss may be consciously acknowledged by the reality has yet to 'sink in' fully. Evidence of this can be seen in many of the common grief reactions noted earlier in this chapter. Hallucinations, feeling the presence of the deceased, dreams and daydreaming about the deceased, holding on to possessions of the deceased, perhaps even visiting spiritualists, can indicate that the loss has not yet been fully accepted. The bereaved person is responding as if they believe the loss is not permanent, that the loss is recoverable. However, as this first Task highlights, an essential feature of the mourning process is to accept fully that the loss has occurred and is irreversible. Such acceptance needs to be accomplished at various levels, consciously and unconsciously, intellectually and emotionally. Accepting emotionally that the loss is real connects with the second Task.

Task Two: To Work Through the Pain of Grief. The death of a loved person is likely to provoke intense pain. This pain may be so distressing that the bereaved person may go to great lengths to prevent themselves experiencing it. Once again we can observe that some common reactions to loss can be seen as attempts to avoid the pain of grief. This may well be helpful in the short term. But the second Task is an essential part of mourning and will usually not be postponed for long. Hence avoiding reminders of the deceased, perhaps by immediately disposing of possessions, idealising the deceased, keeping busy and distracted, may all keep the pain of grief at bay, but for most people they will be temporary measures.

When the pain of loss is experienced it will often be expressed through crying. Although people will naturally vary in the level of pain they experience, and whether nor not they cry, great emphasis has been put on shedding tears because there is evidence that crying is of particular value in the mourning process. A useful distinction to be aware of is that between crying that is motivated by an attempt to hold on to the lost person, and crying that comes from realising they have gone. In the first type of crying it's as if the mourner is pleading for the deceased not to go, its message is 'don't leave me'. The second type of crying seems not to plead but simply to grieve. This second type of crying – which may be closer to what we mean by the term 'weeping' – can only come once the first Task has been accomplished: the mourner accepts emotionally that the loss has occurred and is irreversible. Some researchers have attempted to describe what is happening physically during these two types of crying. The most consistent difference appears to be that in the first type the crying is tense and anxious in nature. It is nonetheless distressing to witness, but there is a clear sense that the mourner is desperately holding on to the deceased. The second form of crying is a deep sobbing which often appears as if the person has given up hope and collapsed. They may appear to be in despair. They are no longer holding on. It is this second sort of crying which, though distressing to experience and to witness, is believed to be of great help physically and psychologically. It is this deep sobbing which has been termed 'healing tears'. Unfortunately, because such sobbing is painful to witness, relatives or friends of the bereaved person may try to distract them from their grief and thus delay essential work on this second Task of Mourning. As we shall see in chapter 8, various 'complications' can occur in the process of mourning and often the difficulty is with completing this second Task.

Task Three: To Adjust to an Environment in Which the Deceased is Missing. A major loss will bring significant changes to the mourner's life. Worden describes how a major loss leads to the need to make adjustments in at least three areas. The bereaved person will need to adjust to changes in their roles, their sense of self, and their view of the world. The loss of a partner can mean the loss of a companion, a sexual partner, a source of support and comfort, and much more. Adjusting to the changes brought by the loss can mean taking on responsibilities that had previously been taken care of by the deceased. It often means learning new skills and adapting to new roles. It often also means adjusting to the experience of not having needs met. This process can take considerable time, and be a source of resentment felt towards the deceased. It is not uncommon for the mourner to rush into a new relationship to try to fill the gap. However, the process of mourning involves adapting to the changes brought by the loss in such a way that the bereaved person has an opportunity to develop their skills, independence and ability to cope.

A major loss will also require major changes in the mourner's sense of self. Often a great deal of self-confidence, or self-esteem, and as we have noted above, self-identity, can be derived from a significant relationship. With the loss of the relationship, there is a sense in which the survivor's 'old self' also dies. The challenge of learning new skills, taking on new responsibilities, and adapting to new roles, can be seen as part of the wider process of redefining oneself in the light of a major loss.

The third area that often requires significant adjustment is the bereaved person's view of the world. By this Worden is drawing attention to the way a major loss can challenge, or even undermine, our most basic beliefs and assumptions about the world. We may struggle to make sense of our loss, desperately looking for a purpose or meaning in what has happened. Life may appear unjust, cruel, or senseless. These concerns are particularly common when the loss has occurred suddenly and unexpectedly. Everything that seemed stable and reliable may be thrown into question and confusion. The bereaved person's view of the world must somehow accommodate both the reality of their loss, and the pain of their grief.

Clearly the adjustments required in the third Task of Mourning can be very substantial, and can take years to accomplish. As the process of mourning unfolds the bereaved person will realise the meaning, or the significance, of their loss as they experience life without the deceased. This is a gradual and painful process, which will require considerable change on the part of the mourner.

Task Four: To Emotionally Relocate the Deceased and Move on With Life. We have noted that Freud suggested that mourning essentially involves withdrawing emotional investment from the deceased and reinvesting emotionally in a different relationship. Of course this does not mean that the deceased is forgotten, or that the survivor becomes indifferent to their loss. Although it is true that the process of mourning requires that the survivor let go of the deceased, and often the bereaved person will have a sense of saying goodbye to the person they have lost, this does not mean that all traces of the relationship are wiped out. Psychologically, what happens during the process of mourning is that the survivor finds a new place for the deceased in their affections, and simultaneously finds room for others. This is what Worden refers to as 'relocating' the deceased. This is a subtle and important point. Freud's description of 'withdrawing' from the deceased can be misleading. The Task is essentially one of breaking the former attachment to the deceased, as a person 'out there', and forging a new relationship to them in the mourner's 'inner world'. This in turn opens the way to establishing new emotional bonds or attachments with others. Sometimes a relationship is formed to help fulfil some need or role vacated by the deceased. But relationships of this sort are not evidence of work on the fourth Task. It is the emotional investment that is crucial. The test of whether work on the fourth Task has been done adequately is if the bereaved person can love in their new relationship. And as Worden notes the best way of describing the incompletion of the fourth Task is 'not loving'.

One way of looking at work on the Four Tasks is in terms of the notion of 'working through'. Without entering into the details of the development and elaboration of this concept, the basic idea of 'working through' is that certain types of new information, especially if it is very discordant with current feelings, thoughts, and behaviours, takes time to become incorporated into a person's psychological make-up in such a way that feeling, thought and behaviour are brought into harmony. The new information needs to be repeated, or re-presented, in different ways and in different situations so that it 'sinks in', or permeates the person's 'inner world'. The loss of a loved person will influence a very wide range of experiences. Being without the loved person is a fundamental change and will have many ramifications. It takes time for all these implications to 'sink in', and for the impact of the loss to be felt and incorporated into the bereaved person's life. Going over the details, thinking about the loss, experiencing the grief, anger, and emptiness, all takes time. Again 'working through' implies an active process, and emphasises the importance of repeatedly going over the experiences of the loss, again and again and again, until the process is completed. The Four Tasks describe a process in which a person works to recover from the experience of losing someone to whom they were strongly attached. The process involves coping with the pain of loss, and revising fundamental beliefs and assumptions about themselves, other people and the world. This involves work and requires time.

It is also important to note that whether we look at mourning in terms of Phases or Tasks there is rarely a smooth movement from one Phase or Task to another. These accounts do not give us a blueprint, or set of rules, stipulating how mourning should proceed. Personal accounts of mourning often describe 'eruptions', or 'pangs' of grief occurring intermittently, despite the fact that the bereaved person believed they had come to terms with their loss (this is particularly common on significant days, such as the anniversary of the death, the deceased's birthday or wedding anniversary, for example). It is also clear that mourners can experience several Phases, or work on several Tasks, at the same time. Also most people experience aspects of the Phases of Mourning, or struggle with the Tasks of Mourning, repeatedly. The whole process is usually much more chaotic than the neat sequences described above. However, these accounts are useful as guidelines that can help us make sense of what is, after all, a very frightening as well as a very distressing experience.

When does the mourning process end?

In describing mourning as a process comprising Phases or specific Tasks, it is natural to ask at what point the process can be considered complete. Bowlby considers mourning to have ended when the Phase of 'Reorganisation' has been completed. Worden considers the end of the mourning process to occur when the Four Tasks have been accomplished. Given the descriptions of mourning offered by Bowlby and Worden it makes sense to talk of the process of mourning coming to an end, or as some prefer to describe it, of grief being 'resolved'. But it must be emphasised that attempts to give a timetable for the various aspects of mourning have not been supported by research. There are very significant individual differences in the time it takes for the process of mourning to be completed. For some it may take months, others may require several years. Such variations are perfectly normal, and it is quite mistaken to assume that there is a set pattern of responses, which occur according to a fixed timetable, any deviation from which must mean something is wrong, or the person is in some way abnormal.

Although we can think of the process of mourning as coming to an end with, for example, the successful completion of the Tasks of Mourning, in some respects mourning never ends. There clearly can be no return to a position identical to that experienced before the loss. The loss is never recovered. But when the person can talk about their loss without tears and without intense pain and grief, and when they can speak of the good and bad times, and can invest emotionally in others, we can speak of the process of mourning as being completed.

Summary

In this chapter we have compared the experience of losing a loved person to receiving an injury. This injury naturally produces emotional distress, pain and grief. Mourning has been described as a process that is necessary for recovery from the injury of loss. John Bowlby's work on attachment has drawn attention to some key aspects of forming, maintaining and breaking emotional bonds. The study of infants when separated from their mothers has shed light upon various features of an adult's response to loss. Many aspects of grief and mourning can be seen as a desperate attempt to regain what has been lost, and the subsequent realisation that the loss is irreversible. A significant loss also threatens an individual's sense of identity, or sense of self. Recovery from loss involves repairing this damage to the self. Bowlby's description of the Four Phases of Mourning helps us to understand the essential point that mourning is a process of adapting to, or recovering from, loss, involving 'Re-organisation' after a period of disruption and disturbance. William Worden's description of the Four Tasks of Mourning offers us a clear picture of the psychological work that is essential to the process of mourning. Viewing the process in terms of these four Tasks helps us to see what is involved in rebuilding one's inner and outer worlds after a major bereavement.

2 Grief and mourning in Britain

In chapter 1 we considered the way Attachment Theory and ideas about the formation of identity can help us understand our experience of, and reactions to, the loss of someone we love. In this chapter we will look at grief and mourning from a different perspective. Many writers in this field make a distinction between the biological fact of death, and the 'social construction' of death. The expression 'social construction' of death refers to the various ways that different societies, or cultures, understand and respond to death. What a person feels, and what a person does when they suffer a major loss is profoundly influenced by the kind of society in which he or she lives. Some aspects of grief and mourning are universal, that is, apparent in whichever society or culture is examined: for example, the desire to regain what is lost that, as we saw in the last chapter, prompts much of the behaviour characteristic of grief and mourning. However, when we compare different societies, or different cultures, it is apparent that death-related attitudes, beliefs, customs, rituals and myths vary enormously. This variation is noticeable across space (for example comparing Britain with Mexico), and across time (for example comparing Britain in the fifteenth century with Britain in the twentieth century). However we shouldn't assume that everyone living in a particular society or culture will respond to death in the same way. There are significant differences in the way people respond to death even when they are from the same society or culture.

Cultural variations cover every aspect of death and mourning. Concerning the deceased's remains, some cultures seek to preserve the corpse while others destroy it as soon as possible – frequently by fire, sometimes by leaving the body to be consumed by animals. In some cultures a corpse is seen as unclean or dangerous; in others, a source of strength that can be transmitted to the survivors by eating the dead flesh. With regard to the dead person, some cultures fear the dead, others revere them, while others dismiss and forget them. The bereaved can be regarded as objects of pity, or as unclean in some way. The disposal of a body can be a time of grief and sorrow or a time of celebration. For some cultures the appropriate response is to wail in grief, others get drunk to give the dead 'a good send-off', others observe a period of silence and restraint. It has been the case in the past, and remains so today, that there is an extremely wide range of beliefs and practices surrounding the subject of death.

In one sense we are all equal in the face of death; we must all die, regardless of who we are, where or when we live. The biological fact of death – the end of physical activity and the disintegration of the body – is unavoidable. However, the significance of death, what death is understood to be, how loss is experienced and responded to, and even the intensity of grief, are all shaped by social and cultural factors. That is, to a large extent these responses are 'social constructions'. Hence how we experience the loss of a loved person, and how we react to that experience, will depend on more than just biological and psychological factors such as those highlighted in chapter 1. To understand a person's experience of grief and mourning we also need to look at how the society or the culture in which they live deals with the reality of death. In this chapter we will outline some of the social and cultural factors shaping grief and mourning in Britain.

Changing patterns of loss

At present about 600,000 people die in Britain each year. But who are they, and who mourns their death? In 1910, the average life expectancy in Britain was 53.5 years. Deaths in childhood, young adulthood and middle age were common. By 1980, average life expectancy had increased to 73.7 years. In 1987, 79% of those who died in Britain were sixty-five or over; whereas in 1969 the figure was 71%. This means that, despite the fact that at any moment about 25% of adults in Britain will have lost someone close to them within the previous five years, death in young, adult, and middle-aged populations is comparatively rare. For most people growing up in Britain today if bereavement is experienced at all it is most likely to be the loss of an elderly relative. Most people reach middle age without experiencing a major bereavement.

Diseases of the circulatory systems, such as heart attacks and strokes, are the most frequent cause of death in Britain. But in the sixteen to twenty-four age group the major cause of death is road accidents; while the second most common cause of death in this group is suicide. In the case of strokes and heart attacks, the death is likely to occur suddenly, without warning. In the case of road accidents and suicide, the death is not only usually unexpected, it is also often violent. About 50% of deaths in Britain occur suddenly, which means, of course, that the bereaved in these situations have no time to prepare themselves to face the loss.

The figures given in the above two paragraphs concern the population as a whole. But there are in fact very significant class differences in life expectancy and cause of death. *The Nation's Health* report in 1988 noted that: 'The expectation of life for a child with parents in social class V is about eight years shorter than for a child whose parents are in social class I.'; and further, that 'social class differences in death rates have widened almost continually since 1951'. 'We estimate that annual excess avoidable deaths in the manual worker classes in men and women aged 16-74 in 1979-83 was 42,000.'

Suicide was de-criminalised in 1961. Although suicide may no longer be a crime in Britain it is still condemned, now in psychological rather than legal terms. This is in fact a rather unusual attitude. Many cultures have had a more positive attitude to suicide. In Europe the Greeks and Romans, even the Christians until the sixth century, endorsed the view that suicide in certain situations could be both a rational and a noble act. By contrast, in modern Britain there seems to be a very strong belief that anyone who chooses to end their life must be mentally ill. Nonetheless, in 1989 there were 4,361 people in Britain who committed suicide. Suicide rates in all groups are increasing. One startling figure, for example, is that from 1980 to 1990 there was a 71% increase in the suicide rate for young males (aged 20 to 24). These are official figures. The real number of suicides is probably considerably higher, as coroners are reluctant to give a verdict of suicide unless there is very clear evidence that the deceased deliberately took their own life. Estimates vary but the number of attempted suicides each year in Britain may currently be approximately 20,000. For someone bereaved through suicide there is, in addition to the pain of loss, the added burden of social stigma. Such stigma frequently leaves the mourner feeling rejected, not merely by the person who has killed themselves, but also by the wider social network that often has so little understanding or tolerance of these situations.

Being comparatively rare and unexpected – and, in the case of road accidents and suicide, often violent – deaths in the younger age groups are likely to be experienced as a catastrophic event in the life of those close to the deceased. Some researchers have also emphasised that there seems to be some generally held beliefs in all 'developed' societies that death simply should not occur in younger age groups, that such deaths are always preventable, and that death should only occur in old age. It is only in old age that death can be regarded as 'natural' or 'timely'; and that death in younger age groups is always 'unnatural', 'untimely', and 'tragic'. It may well be the case that such beliefs add to the burden of grief. For example, parents losing a teenage son in a road accident must face the fact that such deaths are comparatively rare: they will doubtlessly feel it should never have happened, and they may agonise over the reasons for such a calamity. 'Why us? What have we done to deserve this?' Such questions invariably follow loses that are unusual or 'untimely'. Despite their relatively infrequent occurrence, these situations have become the epitome of catastrophic loss – often figuring in media portrayals of family tragedy.

We are perhaps less aware of the fact that elderly people often suffer multiple bereavements. Although some research suggests that generally elderly people appear to suffer lower levels of distress when they lose a partner than younger persons, the process of growing old itself involves a progressive sequence of losses, each of which can legitimately be described as a bereavement. Also individuals vary and it cannot be assumed that the death of a partner with whom someone has shared fifty years of their life will be less disruptive, less 'tragic' and easier to come to terms with, than the loss of a partner in younger age groups.

Patterns of loss have been crucially altered by changes that have occurred in families and relationships in the course of the twentieth century. From the beginning of the century to the present the average completed family size (which only includes children who survived the birth process) has fallen from six to two. It was not unusual in large families at the beginning of the century for some of the children to die. It may be argued that the impact of losing an only child is likely to be a different experience from that of the death of a child in a family of twelve. As noted above, the death of a young child is rare and likely to be outside the range of experience of other family members, friends or neighbours. Research into the ways in which bereaved people have been helped to cope with their loss has consistently noted that mourners find it particularly helpful to be with someone who has sustained a similar type of loss. Although not specifically trained to help people cope with bereavement they are often seen as 'experts' because of what they have experienced. But clearly as the event becomes progressively rarer, there will be fewer such 'honorary experts' available to offer support.

As families have tended to become smaller they have also tended to become more dispersed. Teenagers often leave home and become independent, perhaps cohabiting, at a younger age, and elderly people often live alone. Studies of the composition of households (the number of people actually living together) reveal a clear trend towards smaller units. Notably between 1969 and 1987 the number of people living alone doubled. These changes influence the type of loss that is likely to be experienced, the network of relationships that is likely to be disrupted by the loss, and the level of social support that is likely to be available to mourners. The term 'social support' refers to the extent to which the network of relationships a person has can respond with various types of help and encouragement in times of stress or crisis. Many researchers have noted that the behaviour or relatives, neighbours and friends (potential sources of social support) has a crucial impact on the course of mourning (a topic we will examine in more detail in chapter 7).

A person's relationships, and hence their social support, will be influenced by many factors. However, there appears to be a trend towards forming or maintaining fewer close relationships. Changes in employment and mobility (the rate at which people change jobs or move home) appear to be increasing. These factors contribute to the erosion, some would argue the disintegration, of communities, and hence of relationship networks. It is often said that communities are not as 'tightly knit' as they used to be. That is, the connections between individuals in the community are much looser, the relationships more casual and more superficial. Values such as individualism, competitiveness, acquisitiveness, material and social advancement, and self-interest (values that have taken on the features of a religious dogma over the last decade) also tend to erode a sense of community.

Such changes have had a major impact on the experience of bereavement, in that loss appears to have become progressively more of an individual crisis. Any particular loss is likely to impact on fewer people now than in the past. Communities (if that is the right term) often seem peculiarly immune to the loss of individual members. Many people in Britain experience the death of a loved one as a very private, and a very isolating event. A common assumption appears to be that mourning is the affair of close family members. In other words communal grief has diminished.

John was in his mid-twenties when his father died of a heart attack. He had been working in Manchester for several years, and had found it difficult to visit his family in Glasgow. Although he was able to take two weeks off work to be with his family and attend the funeral, on his return to Manchester he felt isolated and near despair. John had enjoyed his work and had made friends but he felt that his grief 'belonged back in Glasgow, there's no room for it here'. Colleagues and friends appeared to give a strong message that he had had two weeks to recover, and that while he might take a week or so to get back into his routine he should be able to carry on as before. For John there seemed to be no point of contact, no connection, between his background in Glasgow and his life in Manchester. As a result he felt isolated and, as he put it, 'uprooted', and unable to mourn his loss adequately.

John's experience illustrates the point that with greater mobility, and the increasing dispersal of families, a person may be bereaved through the death of a relative or friend living some distance away, perhaps in another city. When this occurs it is usually a very isolating experience because the community where the bereaved person lives, not knowing the deceased, will not experience a sense of loss. Having had no connection with the deceased often makes it very difficult to respond to the mourner's grief and as a result sources of social support may be very limited. The mourner may experience their grief as conspicuously out of place in an environment that, in essence, does not recognise the loss. Such dispersal and dislocation has contributed to the isolating aspect of grief which can leave the bereaved person feeling deeply ashamed of their feelings and anxious to hide the pain of their loss.

In this section we have noted some of the factors that have influenced the patterns of loss in Britain. The relationships that are severed by death have changed profoundly in the course of this century. Who dies, and who is bereaved, have changed as a result of increased life expectancy, changes in the cause of death, smaller family size, greater dispersal of families, and weakening of community ties. Smaller families and lower mortality rates have meant both less exposure to death in families, and a greater impact of the loss: an impact that many of us are ill-equipped to deal with. With limited experience of the reality of death perhaps it is not surprising that many of us find the subject peculiarly difficult to deal with, and that we find it hard to respond in helpful ways to someone who is dying, or who has been bereaved.

The decline in death-related ritual

At present about 80% of deaths in Britain occur in a hospital or other institution, compared to 57% in 1973, and less than 50% in 1960. Death and its aftermath have become thoroughly medicalised and professionalised. Illness, death and mourning are the domain of various professionals: doctors, nurses, therapists, funeral directors, clergy, registrars, etc. For many people illness and death have been taken out of the hands of communities and placed in the hands of professionals. We have many accounts describing how in the past elaborate procedures associated with funerals and mourning were carried out by family and members of the community. Exactly what should be done, how and when, and who should carry out the task were all clearly prescribed. These roles and functions are now the prerogative of professionals. These skills and this knowledge no longer reside in communities. Most of us are left feeling confused and inadequate in the face of loss: 'What can we say? What can we do?' It's perhaps not surprising people often stay away and the bereaved person is left to struggle with their grief in private.

Overall there appears to have been a progressive decline in the observance of ritual and mourning customs, a decline that some researchers trace back to the First World War. It has often been noted that the Victorian era was a period of the 'celebration of death'. This celebration was apparent, for those who could afford it, in very elaborate funeral and mourning ceremonies and rituals. In the course of this century the rituals and customs associated with funerals and mourning have declined. Why this has happened is a matter of considerable dispute. It has been suggested that the decline in death-related ritual has occurred since the First World War as a result of the huge losses sustained in the war. Most families in Britain lost a relative in the war and the sheer scale of such losses led to a decline in funeral customs. Others have argued the opposite: that death-related ritual declined early in this century as a result of the reduction in death rates brought about by improved control of disease. The argument being that as death became less likely in younger age groups, bereavement was less traumatic, and hence the need for ritual was reduced.

Although the death rates appear to be important in some way, researchers have pointed to other changes that have affected death-related ritual. For example, towards the end of the last century the Victorian 'celebration' of death changed to a 'glorification' of death, particularly of dying in battle. Funeral rites reflected this glorification of death. But during the First World War large numbers of bodies were never recovered and this required changes in funeral ritual. Memorial monuments developed as a way of remembering the dead. Also, the horrors of the Great War seriously undermined the idea that it was 'glorious' to die for one's country and this was reflected in funeral ritual, which became much less ostentatious. Although the public rituals and tributes to the dead of the Second World War were similar to those of the First World War, the idea so dominant in Victorian England that dying for one's country was 'glorious' was much less prevalent. As the idea of the 'glorious' dead declined so too did the emphasis placed on memorial and ritual.

Some researchers have suggested that the decline in formal religious observance is the key factor in the decline of death-related ritual. Within Christian belief death is a significant event that, though entailing loss, also contains hope. The central image of Christianity the crucifixion – places death at the heart of belief, and the image of the crucifixion itself contains the hope of resurrection. In this system of belief death is confronted, understood and transcended. Traditional funeral services in Britain have reflected these beliefs. But, it is argued, as these beliefs have become progressively less compelling, ritual based upon them has declined.

Another line of argument has questioned the belief that funeral services and rituals are helpful to the mourners. It is suggested that death-related ritual has declined because it has become progressively less helpful. It is often assumed that funerals and death-related rituals play an important part in mourning, that they help the bereaved come to terms with their loss. But how helpful are they? It was noted in chapter 1 that two crucial features of the process of mourning are accepting the reality of the loss and experiencing the painful feelings provoked by the loss. Arguably funerals help with these two important tasks of mourning. For some the funeral service brings home the reality of the loss. As one sixty-year-old father said of the funeral of his son, who had died in a road accident: 'I hadn't really accepted that he had gone until the service. It was when the coffin was taken behind the curtain for cremation that it hit me. That's when I broke down'. However, some mourners do not feel the funeral helps in coming to terms with their loss. The remarks of one forty-five-year-old widow are not uncommon: 'The funeral was the worst part of it, I just wanted to get it over with. I felt so embarrassed. There's nothing anyone can say, everyone feels awkward, what's the point of it?' It is important to acknowledge that, while it is often assumed that death-related ritual is helpful to the bereaved, that in some way it facilitates and assists the process of mourning, this is by no means true for all people.

We have noted that while it does appear to be the case that death-related ritual has declined in Britain the reasons for this are a matter of dispute. An argument that is sometimes advanced is that the decline in death-related ritual is merely a reflection of the strong tendency for 'developed' societies to attempt to deny the reality of death. It is argued that in countries like Britain death is a taboo subject.

Is death taboo in Britain?

In 1955, sociologist Geoffrey Gorer wrote: 'At present death and mourning are treated with much the same prudery as sexual impulses were a century ago'. To claim that death is our society's 'great taboo' is to say that for us the subject of death is not merely avoided, it is, in various ways and through various measures, prohibited. A popular image of the Victorian attitude to sexuality involves severe constraints on what would be acceptable speech and behaviour on the topic of sex, the whole subject being a source of embarrassment and guilt. Gorer argues that death has replaced sex as our society's central taboo.

Similarly the French historian Philippe Ariès has written in great detail about the very rapid rate of change in social attitudes to death over the last one hundred years. He argues: 'In the course of the twentieth century an absolutely new type of dying has made an appearance in some industrial societies'. He claims that: 'society has banished death', death has been 'driven into secrecy', and that in the face of death 'society no longer observes a pause'.

Gorer and Ariès argue that this taboo has developed largely because of the decline in religious belief and ritual that has occurred in Europe in the course of this century. They claim that all societies are threatened and undermined by the reality of death and so it is necessary to 'tame' or 'detoxify' death. Traditionally this has been done through religious belief and ritual. As these traditional methods of 'taming' death have declined, alternative methods have developed, most notably the denial and progressive avoidance of the reality of death. Death has become taboo. Lacking effective methods for 'taming' death, 'developed' societies have sought to banish death. The movement is towards concealment and secrecy, with death becoming progressively less visible. As ritual has declined we talk less about death, grief is not expressed as openly, mourning is less publicly acknowledged. The bereaved are more isolated and more likely to feel shame and guilt. The reality of death has become shrouded in concealment, secrecy, avoidance, shame and guilt: a death in the family is somehow indecent. However, continuing the analogy with sexual taboos, Gorer argues that this denial of death has led to a burgeoning 'pornography of death'. Gorer uses the expression 'pornography of death' to describe the presentation of death in the media. His argument is that while denying the reality of death, we indulge voyeuristically in endless images of war, disaster, murder and destruction. As Gorer wrote in 1965: 'While natural death became more and more smothered in prudery, violent death has played an ever growing part in the fantasies offered to mass audiences'. The progressive avoidance of the reality of death has led to the development of obsessional fantasies about death. Other writers have argued the same point: as a society we deal very badly with death, we deny its reality and become obsessed with death-related fantasy. Further it is argued that as we become more preoccupied with fantasies about death, we become progressively less able to deal with the reality of death. Inevitably, it is argued, this results in serious psychological difficulties when we are confronted with the loss of a loved person ourselves, if we encounter someone who has suffered a major bereavement, or if we are with someone who is dying.

Although the details of this analysis may be disputed, the general point is clearly true. For many people in Britain today, in common with other 'developed' societies, attitudes towards death are deeply contradictory. Death and mourning have become much less visible, or rather, the realities of death and mourning are much less visible, while at the same time the portrayal of death through images and fantasy is ubiquitous. Studies conducted in the 1980s in the United States suggest the average pre-teen child will view 15,000 murders on television and in the cinema. It may be argued that these figures are considerably higher than would be expected in Britain, but nonetheless entertainment here often involves death, whether this is portrayed as exciting, heroic, tragic, or even comic. Victory for the 'good' often involves killing off the 'bad'. Through news media we are continually reminded of death in wars, famine, disease, accidents and murder. We are bombarded by images of death each day. And yet, this familiarity with images and stories about death has developed alongside the progressive reduction in personal contact with death. As we have seen, most people in Britain can expect to live into old age. Deaths among the young and middle-aged are relatively rare. This means that most people in Britain reach middle age without experiencing the loss of a close relative. In addition we have noted that the majority of deaths (about 80%) occur in institutions such as hospitals and nursing homes, which often means that the dying are isolated from others. Hence, people growing up in Britain today are likely to be exposed to many *images* of death but their personal experience of the *realities* of death are likely to be very limited.

Despite the merits of Gorer and Ariès accounts there have been strong criticisms of certain aspects of their work. I will not enter into the details of the various arguments and counter-arguments; I have included their analysis here because the general point has been very widely accepted and is very often repeated, ironically enough, in the media. Generally the criticisms are more about detail, and about how extensive the taboo is. It has been suggested that death is taboo in certain institutions or professions, such as in hospitals or among doctors and nurses, because these are involved in the industry of saving life, hence death represents failure. Others have suggested that there was a powerful taboo on death when Gorer first reported on the subject in the 1950s, but that over the last thirty years the taboo has been lifted. Still others point out that death has indeed become less visible, mainly because of the changing patterns of mortality in Britain and because of the decline in ritual. However, as death is less visible, it is also less disruptive. It is not that death has become a source of shame and guilt, it is more that it is less important. These and similar view suggest that the claim that death is a taboo subject in Britain has been overstated, and may only be true of particular groups, or particular circumstances. Clearly the picture is a complex one, but one idea that has been persistently emphasised since Gorer published his early studies, is the claim that death will always be problematic because everyone has a deep and abiding fear of their own death. Indeed, some have argued that the fear of death, or fear of personal annihilation, inevitably pervades our individual lives, and society as a whole. In the next section we will consider if this claim is true.

The fear of death

Many writers have claimed that there is a universal fear of death. Everyone, it is argued, fears their own death. This fear is assumed to be innate and, as fear of death prompts defensive action in the face of danger, it is claimed such fear is essential for survival. The German philosopher Martin Heidegger argued that everyone naturally fears their own death but most people go to great lengths to avoid or deny the fact that one day they will die. Heidegger argues, in his regrettably tortuous prose, that we accept 'one dies', but not that 'I die', hence: 'Being-toward-death is essentially anxiety', and, 'the one does not allow the courage for anxiety of death to rise', 'the one brings about a continual putting at ease about death'. In other words we may recognise others must die, but we strive to deny the inevitability of our own death. It is through self-deception that the fear of death is kept at bay.

Sigmund Freud, in a paper published in 1915, gave an alternative view. Freud claimed the First World War had disrupted 'our previous relation to death', which had been one of 'insincerity'. Previously 'we were ready to declare that death was the necessary end to all life', and that death is 'natural, undeniable, and unavoidable'. However, in reality death was denied, pushed out of awareness, 'we have shown an unmistakable tendency to push death aside, to eliminate it from life'. The war, with its massive loss of life, challenged this avoidance – what Freud called 'this insincerity'. However, Freud believed that with respect to our own death denial was inevitable because: 'one's own death is beyond imagining'. And, 'at bottom, nobody believes in his own death', or more precisely: 'In his unconscious, every one of us is convinced of his immortality'. Because of this inability really to conceive of our own death, Freud believed that what we consider to be the fear of death is really fear of something else. That is, fear of death is a mask for a more fundamental anxiety. No one really fears their own death because no one really believes they will die. Of course we can conceive the loss of a loved one, and this may provoke fear, but that is not the same as conceiving that 'I will die'.

Heidegger and Freud both claim most humans prefer not to face death. For Heidegger, the denial and avoidance stems from an unwillingness to face the inevitable dread that realising 'I will die' would provoke. For Freud, people do not acknowledge the reality of their own eventual death because they cannot conceive of such a thing.

These two perspectives have been extremely influential, but they have also been challenged by writers arguing that both views are seriously flawed. For example, American philosopher Walter Kaufmann rejects both Heidegger's view that the fear of death is universal, and Freud's view that our own death is inconceivable. Kaufmann cites numerous examples of people apparently accepting their own death without fear. One well-known example that Kaufmann discusses is that of Japanese suicide pilots during the Second World War, who considered death in combat to be not only a great honour but also highly desirable.

So, according to Kaufmann, neither the fear of death nor the inconceivability of death are universal. However, he does note that the fear of death is certainly very widespread. Kaufmann argues that this fear is largely a product of particular cultures, and is most apparent in societies influenced by Christianity. He suggests that fear of death may be prompted by fear of Judgement. But is this correct? Is it true that religious belief, in particularly Christianity, can increase fear of death?

Research carried out in the 1950s did show higher death anxiety among religious people. But recent work has looked more closely at the relationship between fear of death and religious belief. It appears that there is little or no difference in degree of anxiety about death between people with high or low levels of religious belief and practice. However, those with moderate levels of religious belief and practice appear to experience particularly high levels of death-related anxiety. These findings need to be interpreted carefully, but it seems that people experience greater death-related anxiety when they are uncertain about the significance of death.

An examination of exactly what it is that provokes the fear of death reveals a wide range of concerns. For example, suffering, pain, the unknown, extinction, leaving things undone, distress cause to survivors, and fear of punishment have all been cited as major causes of death-related anxiety. Most often it is separation from loved ones that is considered to be the most distressing aspect of death. An important distinction that needs to be borne in mind is that between fear of death and fear of dying.

Often it is particular aspects of dying that are feared – for example, if the death is slow and painful; or unexpected, thus preventing saying goodbye to loved ones. But there is wide individual variation, and it is clear that 'fear of death' covers a wide range of distinct anxieties, uncertainty about the nature of death being a major one. Hence on the basis of research conducted so far, Kaufmann's claim that Christianity is responsible for increasing people's fear of death appears to be partly true, but we need to acknowledge the wide range of anxieties surrounding death that appear to have little to do with Christian doctrine.

An examination of children's fears shows children are often preoccupied with death. Although it remains a matter of controversy, evidence suggests that by about the age of three children develop a fear of their own death. However, up to about five years, children imagine death to be some kind of journey, or a long sleep. Between about five and eight, children continue to be preoccupied with and frightened of death. But death is imagined to be something or someone who 'comes to get you'. Death is a 'bad person', who is threatening, but also can be avoided. It is after about nine years of age that children seem to become less preoccupied with death, and fears of death diminish. Children's idea of death then approaches that of adults in their family.

Among adults some people seem to be relatively free of fears of death, particularly those in older age groups. In some cases this may be a refusal to accept the reality of death. As Freud noted: 'We regularly emphasize the accidental cause of death, the mishap, the disease, the infection, the advanced age, and thus betray our eagerness to demote death from a necessity to a mere accident'. We can deny death in many ways. Cultural avoidance of the reality of death can be seen in many areas. For example, attempts to thwart the ageing process and an obsession with youth, health and beauty reveal our cultural anxieties and distaste for old age and death. The celebration of youth is matched by the denigration of old age. But this reluctance to face death should not be taken as universal and absolute, as some are inclined to do. Many people are able to accept the inevitability of death, and in some cases to welcome it. Death can be not just an enemy, a horror to be avoided, but a comforter, a goal and a consummation.

It appears that most writers in this field would accept
Kaufmann's view that both Heidegger and Freud were mistaken. Although we can conceive of our own death, fear of death
is not inevitable or universal. However, fear of death does
appear to be common in Britain and doubtlessly contributes to
our difficulties in facing and dealing with death when it comes
to those close to us, or indeed when it comes to ourselves.
Although the picture is a complex one it seems that we are likely
to experience greater problems coming to terms with death
when we lack familiarity with bereavement, when we try to
deny the fact that we too must die, and perhaps when acceptable ritual is not available. But perhaps the most significant
factor is that fear of death is increased when the subject provokes strong feelings of powerlessness and uncertainty. That is,
when there is uncertainty about the nature or meaning of
death.

Does death have meaning?

The experience of bereavement is profoundly influenced by the
meaning the bereaved person gives to death. But death has
many possible meanings. The meaning of death is fluid: it has
had different meanings at different times. Death can have a
very different significance even for people living at the same
time and in the same place. In this and the following section we
will consider both how attitudes to death have changed over
recent centuries in Britain, and also the variation in attitudes
towards death in contemporary Britain.

The historical account given here is based largely on the work
of French historian Philippe Ariès and Austrian theologian
Ivan Illich. Both argue that significant changes in European
attitudes to death have occurred over the last five hundred
years. Illich distinguishes between 'primitive death', 'natural
death' and 'contemporary death'. In the 'primitive' view death is
seen as the result of the deliberate intention of some evil being.
Death could be brought about by witchcraft, evil spirits, angry
gods, dead ancestors, or the spell of an enemy, but in each case
the death was not accidental or 'natural'. The person was
regarded as having been killed deliberately. Further, regardless of the specific cause, death was usually seen as a transition

to another world. Christianity retained the primitive view of death but with modifications. Death remained the result of supernatural agency, but this was not necessarily evil. In the Christian world death was seen as an enemy that had been defeated. The Apostle Paul wrote of death as the 'last enemy' over which Christ had been victorious: 'Death where is thy sting?' In the Christian view death could mean liberation from a state of suffering into a condition of bliss. As such death could be a blessing. Death was still regarded as being the result of supernatural agency, but it was death brought by the angel of God who was a messenger calling the person to Judgement. 'God took them' meant God literally caused the death of a person and thereby called them to account. In the Christian system death is a transition, a door to paradise or a door to hell; or, according to Catholic theology, the opportunity to be cleansed of sin may be offered through a period of purgatory. So 'primitive death', though have many variations, essentially sees death as being caused by a supernatural agency, and as being a transition to another world. This view was dominant in Europe until the fifteenth century.

During the fifteenth century significant changes occurred in European attitudes to death, especially with respect to the cause and significance of death. Illich illustrates these changes by describing changes in popular customs, in particular in what is known as the Dance of the Dead. In Britain, as in other parts of Europe, the Christian church had attempted to eradicate or reform various pagan practices from the fourth century onwards. For a thousand years the Dance of the Dead had been performed in cemeteries. As Illich notes, the Dance was 'a pagan tradition in which crowds, naked, frenzied, and brandishing swords, danced on the tombs in the churchyard'. Death itself being closely linked with renewal, rebirth, and new life, the dance was an expression and celebration of life itself. The dancers danced, as it were, with the dead, in celebration of new life. However by the late fourteenth century the meaning and significance of these dances had changed. Paintings from this period show the dancers dancing, not with the dead in general, but with a corpse that is the mirror image of themselves. Each person, regardless of status, is dancing with their own death. As Illich notes: 'From dancing with dead ancestors over their graves, people turned to representing a world in which everyone dances through life embracing his own mortality'. Prior to this, representations of the death on monuments usually portrayed them in the prime of life, essentially ageless. In the fifteenth century the dead were often portrayed in a state of decay. By the following century death had come to be represented as a skeleton, hence without personal features. Commenting on the woodcuts of the *Danse Macabre*, published by Hans Holbein in 1538, Illich writes: 'The dance partners have shed their putrid flesh and turned into naked skeletons. The representation of each man as entwined with his own mortality has now changed to show his frenzied exhaustion in the grip of death painted as a force of nature'.

Death appears to have changed from something imposed from outside, as a result of the will of a supernatural being, whether evil or benevolent, to a 'natural' and inevitable part of the human condition. The idea of death as the start of new life, death as transition, also appeared to be on the wane. During the sixteenth century death came to be regarded as primarily the end of life, the last act rather than the beginning of a new existence and the start of the Judgement of God. Death, represented by a skeleton, appears as an autonomous figure, not the messenger of God, or agent of the devil. Death is also no longer a reality to which we are intimately related throughout life in a deeply personal way: it is now a universal executioner. Death had become an impersonal, egalitarian force that levels everyone equally. Death does not have a reason to take a particular life; death is merely executing a law that applies to everyone regardless of status. In the sixteenth and seventeenth centuries a morbid preoccupation with death and the afterlife developed, as if people were struggling to make sense of death in the face of the decline of the religious world-view.

Illich argues that these changes have paved the way for a transition from 'primitive death' to 'natural death'. The idea of 'natural death' gradually became dominant in Europe from the fifteenth century and has assumed a number of guises. Initially 'natural death' involved seeing death as an intrinsic part of life rather than an act of God or of evil spirits. Later 'natural death' involved a view of death as an impersonal force of nature. The image of the 'grim reaper' captures this 'force of nature' view. But with the rise of modern medicine in the eighteenth century a new image of 'natural death' developed. To die 'naturally' came to mean to die without an identifiable disease or cause.

Disease came to be seen as preventable or curable, at least in principle, and in some way 'unnatural'. A view developed that saw all death from disease as premature, or 'untimely'. Although disease came to be seen as the enemy that threatens to take life, the nineteenth century saw a number of alternative viewpoints. For some people certain diseases came to acquire a romantic image. Tuberculosis, for example, was seen as the illness of sensitive and talented people. The pale, gaunt features of one suffering from tuberculosis were even regarded as attractive. The illness and the resulting death were romanticised. Other forms of death came to be seen as noble and even desirable. To die fighting for one's country, or a noble cause, especially in a foreign land, became a common romantic theme.

In the twentieth century the First World War seems to have punctured the idea that dying in battle for one's country was 'glorious'. Disease is rarely romanticised and religious belief and practice has declined. What Illich calls 'contemporary death' has developed where societies have become highly industrialised and medicalised. Without a framework of assumptions such as has been provided in traditional cultures, death is often experienced as meaningless and arbitrary. Long illness may also appear pointless, and it may be impossible to see any redeeming or ennobling factors in the pain and distress of illness and loss. The idea that suffering can actually be an opportunity for a personal transformation, that pain can actually contribute to the quality of an individual's life may seem absurd.

Care of the sick and dying has been handed over to 'experts'. It is expected that there will be cures for all diseases; disease and death are portrayed as mistakes and tragedies. Death from any cause other than old age is regarded as 'untimely' and 'unnatural'. Such deaths must be someone's fault, someone or something has failed. Someone has been irresponsible or negligent. Death is not seen as a natural feature of life, it is experienced as an alien intrusion, and can only occur because something is wrong. This is one of the features of 'contemporary death' that Illich considers to be a regression back to 'primitive death'. Because someone somewhere must be responsible, blame, anger or guilt often follow. In passing responsibility over to professionals another effect has been the isolation of the dying. Often they are shunned, as are the bereaved. Illness and death are unwanted realities that are seen in terms of tragedy and failure. It is not surprising we find it difficult to talk to the dying or the bereaved. The medicalisation and profession-alisation of death has included the 'normalising' and 'patho-logising' of grief. That is, what is 'normal' and what is 'abnor-mal' (or pathological) to feel and do after losing a loved one are prescribed by 'experts'. Death has shifted from the domain of the spirit to the domain of the flesh. As such, death – the ceasing of physical functions – represents failure. When a doctor says: 'We did all we could', he or she means: 'We failed to keep the person alive'. Illich is critical of many of the changes in attitude towards death in 'developed' countries, and he argues that these changes have left us peculiarly ill-equipped to deal with the realities of dying, death and loss.

Another factor that can add to the pain of bereavement may be the recent emphasis on the supposed significance of psycho-logical factors in physical health in general and terminal illness in particular. In Britain heart disease and cancer cause many deaths each year. It has been suggested that both these ill-nesses are related to factors such as personality, attitudes, characteristic ways of dealing with emotions, quality of rela-tionships, and responses to 'stress'. Despite the fact that re-search has not produced consistent results, the idea that a person is responsible for their illness – in the sense that if they had changed their thoughts, their attitude, their emotions, or their levels of 'stress', they could have avoided the illness – is a very potent and increasingly widespread idea. There are two disturbing features of this situation. First, the evidence sup-porting such claims is very thin indeed. And second, the moral-istic or judgemental implications of such unsupported asser-tions lead to the apportioning of blame, usually to the sufferer themselves (a manifestation of the conveniently comforting activity of 'blaming the victim'). The effect is that not only is a person suffering the discomfort and distress of a serious illness but they are also blamed for their condition. Although such blame may not actually be voiced this moralistic perspective may influence the quality of care provided. The logical outcome of this judgemental stance is to withhold treatment from those perceived as 'irresponsible' and channel resources to 'the wor-thy' whose illnesses are not considered to be their own fault. This attitude is unfortunately prevalent among health workers, both orthodox and complementary. The implication of such views is that if someone dies before they are old and the death has not been caused by someone else (such as through homicide or an accident), the deceased themself must be responsible for their own death. We can all feel more comfortable if we can blame the deceased themself, but it is also easy to see how those who have been bereaved by the loss may blame themselves. The survivors may feel they contributed to the psychological habits of the deceased and therefore contributed to their death. Clearly such beliefs can add immeasurably to the burden of grief.

In considering attitudes to death in Britain today it is important to take note of other trends which have attempted to counteract the negative aspects of 'contemporary death'. In the 1960s and 1970s in the United States and Europe, a movement developed that critically examined contemporary attitudes and practices surrounding death. This 'death awareness' movement has attempted to educate people about the realities of death and to counter the fantasy images of death. Attention has been given to the importance of honesty about the difficult feelings that many of us experience in the face of death. An attempt has been made to create a climate wherein unspoken fears, guilt, shame, and other painful feelings can be openly acknowledged and accepted. This honesty has also extended into the area of religious belief: what does the bereaved person really believe about the meaning of death? Some people find strength through religious belief but others may find their faith is undermined by a major loss. It can be very difficult to face such a crisis of faith, but many have done so and found reserves of strength to help them cope. It has been a key feature of the 'death awareness' movement that all these aspects of death, dying and loss, which previously tended to be avoided, have been brought out into the open.

The hospice movement has made an important contribution to changing attitudes in Britain. Hospices usually provide a range of services including in-patient facilities which involve careful control of pain; out-patient, home-nursing and support teams which can assist the dying and their families or carers; and support for bereaved relatives. Currently there are about seventy hospices in Britain, with a total of about two thousand beds. It is estimated that between forty to fifty thousand families each year are helped by some aspect of the hospice service. Although it is possible to identify a number of models of care underlying the variation in hospice practice, there is also an explicit philosophy that the hospice movement attempts to embody. Dying is seen as a vital part of life, and each person is considered to have a right to die with as much comfort and dignity as possible. Death is not regarded as inevitably tragic. The dying are not shunned. The physical and emotional needs of the dying person are given careful attention while recognising the importance of the individual dying their own death. The hospice movement has also given careful attention to the needs of relatives and friends of the dying person, and the needs of those who have been bereaved. Hospice provisions are largely funded by cancer charities, which reflects the traditional association of the hospice movement with care of cancer patients. However there are various projects underway to extend the hospice philosophy to a wider range of services and patient groups, and to influence attitudes in hospitals, other institutions, and in the community in general.

In contemporary Britain you can in fact find wide variation in attitudes towards death and dying. Death means different things to different people. An important part of this varied picture is the attitude towards death and dying that has been preserved by Britons with differing cultural identities. We will consider this in the next section.

Death in a multi-cultural society

So far we have looked at some of the more important influences on the experience of loss in Britain in general. But there are many other factors influencing the experience of loss for specific groups in Britain. Since the Second World War Britain has developed as a multi-cultural society. In the Middle Ages the idea of the 'Good Death', the view that there is an art or skill to dying that would profoundly influence what happens to the deceased in the afterlife, was commonplace. Such a view has long since passed for many people in Britain. However, Britons who have roots in some non-European cultures have preserved the notion of a 'Good Death', leading to an advantageous condition beyond death.

Some communities in Britain have attempted to retain their traditional practices despite living in a society where the trend is towards abandoning what are often called 'pre-scientific' beliefs, rituals and practices. One example is that of the Hindu community. Many British Hindus have immigrated from India or East Africa. Often people from these countries have had very much more personal contact with death than people living in 'developed' countries. Families in these societies tend to be larger and have higher mortality rates than in Britain. They also have a rich heritage of traditional belief and practice associated with death. Hindus believe in reincarnation: physical death is seen as merely the casting-off of a physical body, following which the soul will be reborn – a process occurring continually until final liberation from rebirth is attained when the individual soul merges with God. The conditions of a person's present life are determined by their karma, that is the deliberate actions of a previous life.

Hindus have a clear view of what constitutes a 'Good Death'. Ideally the person should die after a long life. They should die on the floor (a practice once common in Europe), while Hindu scriptures or the names of God are chanted, and with basil leaf and water from the Holy River Ganges in their mouth. The state of mind at death is thought to be crucial in determining the fate of the soul; hence to be able to read the Hindu holy texts to the dying person is regarded as rendering a great service to them. For Hindus the rituals at death allow the soul to continue its journey, and without such rituals the soul may become stuck, with serious consequences for the deceased and the relatives. If relatives are not present when a person dies, or if they are prevented from performing prescribed rituals, the trauma and loss is greatly increased. For Hindus the days immediately after death are also crucial in determining the fate of the soul: detailed rituals are prescribed to assist the soul on its passage to its next life. In the context of Hindu beliefs the importance of performing these rituals is as crucial for the well-being of the survivors as it is understood to be for the dead. The living have responsibilities to help the dying person have a 'Good Death' and the benefits to the survivors are manifold.

Because Hindus hope the soul of the deceased has gone to God or to a better rebirth, they are encouraged not to grieve excessively. However, the display of emotion, by both men and women, may be considerably more intense than that shown by Britons of Anglo-Saxon origin. As mentioned above most people die in hospital in Britain, and it is unfortunately the case that a lack of awareness of the importance of these rituals to Hindus often creates difficulties. Problems can arise when hospital staff are reluctant to inform relatives that the patient is close to death, or if relatives are prevented from performing the required rituals.

British Moslems are in a similar situation: coming from a rich cultural tradition with comprehensive explanations and observances regarding illness, death and mourning, and having to adapt these to an often uncomprehending and unsympathetic society. For Moslems the manner and time of death is in the hands of God, but there are important obligations that relatives must carry out towards the dying. For example, the state of mind at the point of death is regarded as a crucial factor determining the after-death existence, hence being with the person at the point of death, praying with them, and reciting the kalima (the profession of faith: 'There is no God but God, and Muhammed is the Prophet of God'), are seen as essential obligations that the living must carry out for the dying. This is of great importance for the person dying and for those who face bereavement. Moslems believe that God sends the angel of death to bring the spirit out of the dead body, but at the same time the Devil tries to mislead the dying person. Chanting and prayer are to help the dying person resist this Satanic assault. Moslems also believe that after an initial period of dwelling with God the good soul is returned to remain by the body until the resurrection. Attachment to the body, or being ill-prepared, hinders this journey to God in the company of the angel. An important act of devotion, usually carried out by close relatives, is the preparation of the body for burial. This involves washing the body and wrapping it in a shroud. Internment ideally takes place within twenty-four hours. If possible the corpse is laid so that it will face Mecca, the Holy city, when it rises from the grave at the resurrection.

Once again, as with those in the Hindu community who wish to preserve their traditional beliefs and practices, British Moslems face the difficult task of trying to integrate their traditional practices with current medical and hospital procedures, which are often inflexible and intolerant. The process of adjustment to conditions in Britain is a challenge to these communities. Of course the existence of such elaborate beliefs and rituals does not remove the pain of losing someone who is loved. Despite the fact that Hindus and Moslems believe that the individual soul will live on in another form, they too will experience the death of a loved one as a painful loss, just as someone who does not believe in reincarnation or resurrection.

Summary

In this chapter we have looked at some of the changes in attitudes and mourning practices that have occurred in Britain. Grief reactions and the process of mourning have important biological and psychological roots, as we saw in chapter 1. But it is also clear that there have been, and are, considerable variations in the way grief and mourning are experienced and expressed in different cultures and at different times. Social and cultural factors overlap and shape the expression of biological and psychological processes, such as the formation of attachments and the development of personal identity.

We have noted that the 'social construction' of death, as distinct from the biological fact of death, is extremely variable. Responses, attitudes, and observances all vary across time and place, and between individuals. Attitudes towards death, ideas about the cause of death, fear of death, beliefs about the meaning of death, belief in afterlife, what are appropriate observances and mourning rituals, whether the living can help the dead and whether the dead can influence the living, attitudes to suicide, and our understanding of illness have all varied considerably. In view of this variation it is simply not possible to stipulate what a person should or should not feel or do when they lose someone they love.

3 Grief and mourning in childhood and adolescence

In this and the following chapter we will consider the impact of major bereavement on different age groups. Throughout it is important to note that the way a person is affected by a major loss will be influenced by many factors. These include the personality of the bereaved person; their previous experience of loss; the nature of the relationship between the survivor and the deceased; the way in which the loss occurs; and how the loss is responded to by other family members. The information in this and the following chapter provides a glimpse of some of the issues and problems that can arise in particular situations of loss. No attempt is made to present rules about how particular losses 'should' be responded to, or how they 'should' affect those who have been bereaved. As noted in chapter 1 there are no such rules. But finding out how others have been affected by particular losses can often help take some of the fear out of mourning and make the process of adapting to loss a little easier to bear.

Loss during the first two years

It was noted in chapter 1 that even from the first weeks of life the infant engages with his or her mother, or primary care-giver. Towards the end of the first year of life an infant will search for his or her mother when she is absent, and will display unmistakable attachment behaviour, as described in chapter 1. During the first year of life a significant loss usually means loss of the mother, and the main impact of such a loss will be through the disruption of mothering. If a mother dies suddenly the continuity of care may be temporarily interrupted. Infants will respond to such disruptions with evident distress. Where there is warning that the care of the infant will be interrupted, perhaps through the mother's illness, the role of mothering can be taken over by someone else with minimum disruption to the child. Although bonding and attachment occur very early in a child's life, the impact of a mother's death can be significantly reduced if physical and emotional care of the child is provided in a consistent and reliable way.

The impact of loss on an infant can be considerable if the mother suffers a bereavement. Infants are very sensitive to their mother's moods and reactions and if there is a death in the family the mother's response to the loss will be 'picked up' by the infant. A mother's grief can exert a profound influence on her child. So even though an infant will not have formed relationships with members of the wider family circle, any deaths occurring in this wider network of relationships can affect the infant though the response of the mother. Once again, to minimise the impact of such losses continuity of physical and emotional care is essential. It is often helpful if the provision of such care can be shared by family members in order to allow the bereaved mother the space to mourn her loss.

Estimates vary, but it has been argued that the very earliest manifestations of grief can appear in infants as young as four to five months. But it is during the period six months to two years that the beginnings of grief and mourning unmistakably appear. If a parent dies in this period the infant will search, and, when able, ask for the lost parent. The prolonged absence of the parent often leads to the protest-despair-detachment sequence which, as we noted in chapter 1 often follows separation. Because the child has not yet learned to control or disguise strong feelings, grief in this period will be clearly demonstrated. Although there is a more overt display of grief, the infant during this period is experiencing and responding to grief in essentially the same way as older children.

Loss during the years two to five

From about the age of two children develop an understanding of the meaning of death. Often this is through contact with nature: death of animals, birds, insects, even flowers. Researchers have noted that many two-year-olds are more fascinated than horrified by death, but this develops around the age of three into a fear of death. By about three a child will understand that he or she will also die. Games involving death ('cowboys and indians') are common, and three- to five-year-olds not only think abut death and injury, they often appear preoccupied with these subjects. Children realise death means the end of life and often become very concerned about the causes of death. They tend to view death as the result of someone's action, that is when people die it is assumed they must have been killed by someone. Children of two and three see death in very literal terms. For example, death means going to sleep forever, or going away to a particular place. The child may fear growing up because they equate growing old with dying. Fears of going to sleep are also common, as sleep can easily be associated with death. Statements like 'he fell asleep in death' may be taken literally, inducing dread of sleep.

Many parents feel children at this young age should be told comforting stories about death. If a death occurs in the family the child may be told that the person has 'gone away for a while', or 'gone to be with Jesus'. In the face of the child's fears of their own death the child may even be told that they will not die. Stories designed to 'protect' the child are seldom helpful. If someone in the family is ill it is best to be truthful about this. Similarly if a member of the family dies the child will be helped more by being told the truth. Comparisons with death in nature may be helpful. For example if a pet has died, or even when flowers or plants die, the child of this age understands what it means. If the family does not have a religious focus it is rarely helpful suddenly to introduce the idea of heaven. If the parents do not believe in an afterlife in this way the child is likely to be confused by talk of angels and God and heaven.

The child will want to ask questions and it is best if these are answered honestly. This may be very difficult, especially when the adults in the family are struggling with their own grief. But the young child is part of the family, and will need to express his or her own grief. Children are often excluded from the funeral or from seeing the deceased's body. They may also be given very unclear messages about the finality of death. If a child in this age group experiences a bereavement it is likely to be sudden. Frequently they are not told for some time, and often they are told the person has 'gone away' with the implicit – and sometimes explicit – idea that they will return. If a parent has died and the remaining parent remarries the child will have to struggle to understand why.

Helen's husband died in his mid-thirties, leaving her with three young children, aged two, three and five. Helen found it extremely difficult to adapt to her loss and relied on her own mother, who lived with the family, to look after the children. Helen found her own reaction to the loss to be so frightening and distressing that she felt it vital to protect the children from what had happened. Hence the children were told that their father had had to go away but would return, and that their mother was ill, and needed to spend time resting in bed or away at her sister's. Helen and her mother intended telling the children the truth when they were 'old enough to cope with it'. Although their intentions were to spare the children the pain of loss, such stories invariably made an extremely unfortunate situation worse. Children are not so easily deceived. Helen's own grief and the children's progressively unmanageable behaviour persisted for several years until help for the whole family was sought.

Sometimes a new baby will be described as a dead brother or sister that has returned. The question of the finality of death is a major preoccupation for children in this age group and it is best if they are told the truth: that the dead person will not return. From around the age of two and a half children will respond to loss in ways very similar to adults. It is important to recognise that children do feel grief, and do mourn, and hence will need to be included in the family's mourning – not excluded to 'protect them', or because 'they don't understand'. The reluctance of adults to include young children may be because their own grief is so overwhelming they cannot begin to see the young child's grief as well. But if the family is to come through a major loss without long-term problems for the family as a whole, or individual members of the family, then the children's grief needs to be acknowledged and responded to.

Children of this age group often experience powerful destructive fantasies. Smashing toys or making a mess can be an expression of these destructive feelings. These feelings may well extend to people and be reinforced by parents saying 'you're killing me', or 'you'll be sorry when I'm gone'. These statements can give the child the idea that he or she does indeed have the power to injure or kill people. If a parent or brother or sister should then die the child may feel he or she is somehow responsible.

Just like adults, children respond in different ways to loss. As with younger children the familiar pattern of protest–despair–detachment can often be seen when children in the two to five age group lose a parent. Initially the child may be stunned, or apparently unaffected, unable to understand what has happened. The young child may repeatedly ask where the deceased is, or when they will return. Often the child's play will be focused on death. Again the most helpful response to this will be to acknowledge the questions and gently, and if necessary repeatedly, tell the child the truth. Some children may appear to slip back to an earlier way of behaving (often called 'regression'), by wetting or soiling, being very clinging, wanting to return to bottle or breast feeding, and earlier ways of eating and moving. Alternately the child (most usually boys) may become aggressive and uncontrollable. It can be very disturbing to the surviving parent to be asked repeatedly about their partner who has just died. It can be even more disturbing when the child reacts with angry protest or withdrawal, as this will feel like a rejection. Anger may be expressed towards the dead parent and also towards the survivor. Perhaps the child may blame the surviving parent for the death. In view of the difficulties that can arise it is not surprising that young children are often sent away to stay with relatives if a major loss has occurred in the family. But generally it is more helpful for all concerned if the family can remain together and grieve their loss together.

When a bereaved child withdraws as a way of protecting themself from emotional pain it can appear that the child has adapted to the loss. The family may describe the child as 'coping well' with the trauma, and even consider the child to be 'a great support'. But it is important to recognise that children in the two to five age range will experience the death of a family member as a great loss and will need to mourn their loss just as adults do. When permitted to do so these young children can express the pain of the loss and their yearning for the return of the deceased. They can also accept the finality of loss.

The great dilemma facing a parent who has lost their partner is that while they may want to help their children they feel paralysed by their own grief, and by the fact that they simply cannot provide what the child will often repeatedly and without inhibition ask for: the return of the lost parent. A further difficulty is that in families where there is more than one young child the youngest may be more expressive in both their questioning and their distress. The older child may already have learnt to conceal his or her feelings. In such cases the surviving parent may have their attention repeatedly drawn to the younger child and assume the elder one's relative calm means they have managed to adjust to the loss. The truth may well be that the elder child feels unable to mourn and is blocking off painful feelings in order to cope.

Where a brother or sister has died, this is often less traumatic for a surviving child of this age, as long as the parents are not paralysed by grief and can allow the child his or her own grief and mourning. In situations where the mother's pregnancy has had to be terminated, or has resulted in a still birth, young children will be aware of a period of anticipation and preparation (often being told about a new brother or sister that will soon arrive), which is then followed by grief. It is easy to assume the infant will not be affected by this loss but this would be a mistake. Young children are extremely sensitive to the moods and feelings of parents, and can be deeply affected by their parents' grief.

So for a child in the two to five age group a major bereavement (most notably the death of a parent, or the death of a brother or sister) will be experienced as a significant loss that provokes grief and mourning. They will also need to mourn their loss just as adults do. Unfortunately much of the behaviour that is an expression of grief in the young child will often not be recognised as such. The young child's grief often goes unacknowledged, and unshared. The surviving parent or parents can best help the child by telling them the truth, especially about the finality of death; and by allowing the child's grief and not attempting to deflect it or avoid it by telling stories, or telling them they must 'be strong' or 'grown-up'. As with adults, the grief of a two- to five-year-old can continue for months, even years.

Loss during the years five to eight

During these years children have usually become very skilled at concealing or disguising their feelings, hence many children will try to hide their grief if a major bereavement occurs. As noted in chapter 1 'denial' is a psychological defence. The child may avoid experiencing the pain of loss by not fully accepting the reality of what has occurred. A child practising denial in this way may appear to be coping very well. Especially where a younger sibling is expressing their own grief very openly, the needs of a child in the five to eight range can easily go unnoticed. Where a child between the ages of two to five may persistently ask about the dead parents or sibling, the older child will more usually be silent. Boys may become aggressive and find it difficult to express their sadness and longing for the lost parent. But with encouragement children in this age group will express their feelings about the loss. The essential message they need to hear is that their feelings are acceptable and can be shown within the family. Of course this will be difficult if they have been given strong messages against crying, or against anger, or against sadness, in their early years.

A major problem for children in these years is the stigma of being different. Other children at school may treat them differently – perhaps even mock or abuse them. It is extremely difficult for a child to manage these pressures, but it will help considerably if his or her feelings are acknowledged and accepted in the home. Once again the important thing is to recognise that the child needs to grieve and mourn just as the adult does. He or she will be best helped by openness and honesty, and by the inclusion in the family's expression of grief and mourning. Again the mourning can continue for months or even years.

Graham was eight when his mother died. His father recalled the death of his own mother when he was ten, and how upsetting he found the funeral. To protect him from having to witness the family's grief Graham was sent to stay with the grandparents of a friend on the day of the funeral. Attempts were made to cheer him up and occupy his mind as if nothing was happening, in the belief that he would be helped most if he could be protected from the truth and gradually allowed to get used to his mother's absence. Once again, such well-meaning attempts to lessen the pain of loss are misguided in that they assume that it is better to avoid experiencing the full impact of a loss. But grief is best dealt with by feeling and expressing it, and if at all possible, by doing so in contact with others. There is no way that the loss of a parent can be made innocuous. It is a tragedy that must be faced, and felt, regardless of age. Avoidance merely creates long-term difficulties, as we shall see in some detail in chapter 8. For Graham the pain of his loss was not fully experienced until many years later, when he was in his twenties. As far as possible it is more helpful for children to be included in the family's mourning, than for them to be excluded in the belief that this will protect them from pain.

Loss during the years eight to twelve

From about eight years of age the child's ability to understand what death is and their response to death will have developed to approximately that of an adult. He or she will understand that it is part of the natural life cycle, that he or she will also die, and that death is permanent. Fear of death, and defences against that fear, influence the way a child in this age range will experience a major bereavement.

As children of this age will often have developed a number of relationships beyond the immediate family they may experience the death of someone in this larger social group as a major personal loss. Death will bring into focus the child's own mortality, and is likely to provoke thoughts about the eventual deaths of other family members. Imagining the future without the loved person may be particularly disturbing to the child in this age group. These children will also be in the early stages of establishing an identity and independence beyond the family and a major bereavement will threaten this growing sense of independence. Having gained a measure of control over their feelings, the powerful emotions provoked by death may threaten to overwhelm the child. Shock, anxiety, fear, distress, and confusion are typical responses, which a child may find extremely disturbing. The child's early efforts to behave like an adult may be threatened as the child may feel in danger of being overwhelmed by powerful feelings he or she cannot control. The sense of helplessness that this produces may be fiercely resisted. Again it is common for children in this age group to try to push away their grief and continue as if they are unaffected. Frequently the grief will break through. If this happens it is important that family members accept these feelings, demonstrating that he or she need not feel ashamed of their grief or their feelings of longing and helplessness. In particular these children need to recognise that such feelings are not 'childish'. Children in this age group may go to great lengths to avoid appearing helpless and vulnerable in an effort to preserve what they may consider to be mature and adult responses to loss. Adults can be of great help if they show they can accept their own feelings of distress and helplessness, as well as allowing the child to experience their own grief.

A situation that can be particularly difficult for a parent to deal with is when the child presents a facade of coping, but becomes very irritable with the parent or parents. If the child has lost someone very close – a sibling or a parent – he or she may experience intense and frightening anger. Part of this anger may be connected with a sense that the surviving parent, or parents when a sibling has died, are somehow responsible for the death. The child may not express such ideas clearly and explicitly because they may not be very clear in their own mind. But their anger and their behaviour may express a sense of accusation, or blame, towards the parent or parents. This, of course, can be very confusing and upsetting for family members: instead of sadness and grief, which is expected, the family sees anger.

Difficulties at school will be even more pronounced for this age group than for younger children. The developing sense of independence and formation of relationships outside the family will be of increasing importance and being accepted by peers will be vital to the child's well-being. For boys especially, the thought of appearing childish or weak may provoke deep anxiety, and hence they may try to avoid anything that makes them appear vulnerable. Thus taking time off school or wearing distinctive clothes for a period of mourning can become an excruciating trial for the child, as these things mark him or her out as different. Some school environments may be particularly unsympathetic and the child may be subjected to abuse or ridicule. In such circumstances the child's mourning may be postponed, the priority being survival in the harsh and unsympathetic world of school.

Mark was twelve and had recently started at a new school when his mother died. Although his father thought it best that Mark did not attend the funeral he wanted him to wear a black tie at school as a sign of mourning and respect. Mark was confused by the way he seemed excluded from the family mourning while at the same time expected to display his loss in public on his own. To add to his difficulties he was made a target of abuse and ridicule by other boys in the school. Mark recalled being singled out by the headmaster in front of a large class and asked: 'Why aren't you wearing the proper uniform?' For Mark these and similar experiences greatly added to the burden of his loss. Unfortunately his family, weighed down by their own grief, were simply not aware of the difficulties he was experiencing.

In order to help children in this age group adults need to be sensitive to the extraordinary pressures children in this situation face. Research indicates that many of these children do not have their grief recognised. It is easy for adults to go along with the child's attempts to stifle their feelings and act in what is supposed to be an 'adult' way, especially if the impact of the bereavement has led to major disruption in the family. A child in this age group may be called upon to carry out many 'adult' functions in the home, leaving little room for their own grief and necessary mourning. But it is important to remember that there is no virtue in suppressing grief; the fact that many adults do so is no reason to recommend it, or to consider it a mature way of responding to loss. Adults can help children by showing that they needn't be ashamed of their grief, or the associated feelings, even if these are confusing, and perhaps at times seem unusual.

Although it is the death of a parent that usually has the greatest impact in this age group, the death of a sibling can also be devastating. A major problem can arise where the surviving child feels guilty. Brothers and sisters naturally experience a range of emotions towards each other, including at times intense hostility and rivalry, as well as affection. If a sibling dies, especially if this occurs suddenly, the surviving child may associate the death with their own anger and destructive wishes. The resulting guilt can remain for many years and can interfere with mourning and lead to various difficulties in later life (we will consider some of these difficulties in chapter 8). If the parents' own grief prevents them from fully engaging with the surviving child, and if they are unable to re-establish a sense of joy in their relationship with the child, the feelings of guilt may be increased. The surviving child may assume that the parents preferred the dead child. To avoid this difficulty it is important that the parents remain emotionally accessible to the child – even in their grief. This is very difficult for many parents to do, but is essential if they are to help the surviving child adjust to the loss.

Remaining open to the child emotionally will of course mean that the child will see the parents' own grief. Some have argued that this is not helpful for a child, that the child will be frightened if they see one or both of their parents extremely distressed. The difficulty, of course, is that the child cannot be protected from grief. The issue is: what is the best way to deal with grief? Evidence supports the claim that experiencing and expressing grief with others will ultimately be healing, though no-one pretends this will be anything but painful. For a child it is helpful when their own grief is acknowledged and allowed expression within the family, so that in a real sense the loss is shared.

Changes in the family following a major bereavement affect the process of mourning. In particular, changes in the role of the surviving child can disrupt mourning. One example is where the parent or parents relate to the child as if he or she were a replacement for the child who has died. But another example that can lead to very serious long-term problems is where the surviving child is made a scapegoat – that is, blamed in some way for the death. The parent, or parents, themselves may feel guilty about the death – perhaps it occurred through an avoidable accident – and in such cases the guilt may be assuaged by a subtle (or at times not so subtle) blaming of the surviving child. This will naturally lead to a deterioration in the relationship and disruption of the mourning process. For a child in such a position the loss has been compounded: not only have they lost a parent or brother or sister, they have also lost their former relationship with the surviving parent or parents.

Sarah was ten when she was asked by her mother to take care of her four-year-old brother Tom. They were playing with a ball in the front garden when Tom hit the ball over the hedge. Sarah went out through the gate to retrieve the ball but on her return she did not secure the gate adequately. A little later when Sarah went into the house to get a drink Tom ran out of the garden through the gate. When Sarah returned to the garden she saw the gate was open and Tom was gone. She ran after him and saw him run into the road. He was hit by a motorcycle and died later in hospital. Sarah had always felt that her parents, especially her mother, preferred Tom as he was a boy. But after the accident her relationship with her parents deteriorated and Sarah was convinced they would have preferred her to die rather than Tom, and blamed her for his death. The tangle of feelings in this situation, which included guilt, blame, jealousy, hostility and resentment, served to complicate the grief. The difficulty of adequately mourning such losses is greatly exacerbated by the deterioration in the family relationships

Another major change that can influence mourning is when a surviving parent remarries. Evidence suggests many remarriages are in fact successful, and despite some initial difficulty most children benefit in the long run. But it is important that the new partner is not presented as a 'replacement' mother or father. New relationships have to be formed. An accepting and understanding attitude on the part of the parent can help the child to develop a new relationship with the step-parent. This new relationship is not a copy of the relationship with the parent who has died. Initially the child may resent or reject the new parent, and may experience renewed grieving over the mother or father they have lost. But if this response is dealt with in a caring and sympathetic way new relationships between bereaved children and a step-parent can be successfully developed, with benefits for the whole family.

Loss during adolescence

Adolescence is for many a time of great upheaval. The physical, emotional, and sexual changes which occur during adolescence may be both stressful and distressing for the adolescent. The turmoil of these years may also take its toll on the family. Confusion over identity and vocation, experimenting with new behaviours, risk-taking and rebellion are common during these years, although naturally the extent to which these difficulties will be present varies considerably between individual adolescents. Similarly, families deal with these changes in different ways. However it would be a rare household in which the challenges of adolescence brought no stress to the family. A major issue for adolescents centres around the drive for independence.

Separating from the family, forming sexual relationships, earn-
ing a living and surviving independently, often conflicts with
the desire – which is usually unacknowledged – to remain in the
protected environment of the family. This conflict is related to
another difficulty, that of emotional ambivalence. 'Ambivalence', as we nave noted, refers to having opposing feelings for
the same person. Adolescents often experience both love and
hatred for their family. This conflict can be a major source of
stress for the individual and the family.

When a death occurs in the immediate family – of a parent or
brother or sister – the adolescent faces the enormous burden of
adapting to the changes adolescence brings as well as coping
with their grief and mourning. It is during adolescence that a
child's understanding of death develops to that of an adult. The
adolescent also develops their capacity for criticism and ideali-
sation. Often family members will find themselves on the receiving end of newly-established critical faculties. They may
come to represent everything that the adolescent wants to
reject and rebel against. In contrast pop stars or sports person-
alities may be idealised; they can do no wrong, they are seen as
beyond criticism, almost godlike. Naturally these changes often
produce conflict and stress in the family, and if an adolescent is
bereaved they may find it very difficult to look to their family for
support through their grief and mourning.

In many ways adolescence involves coming to terms with a
series of losses. The changes of adolescence cannot be accommo-
dated without letting go of earlier ways of behaving and relat-
ing. Being a child, and the role of the child, must be left behind.
A new identity must be forged. This process involves numerous
losses. Many adolescents are very anxious to demonstrate that
they are no longer children. They demand to be treated as
adults, and could experience any tendency they may have to slip
into 'childish' ways of behaving as very threatening. This may
be particularly pronounced when in the company of their peers.
As we have noted, grief and mourning often does involve a kind
of 'regression'; that is, a tendency to revert to more dependent,
emotional behaviour, in which experiences of helplessness and
perhaps clinging are reawakened. We may typically associate
this type of response with children. This regression is perfectly
normal, and in many ways helpful. It is a sign of maturity that
this temporary state of 'Disorganisation' (as John Bowlby calls

it) can be permitted. But it is very difficult for many adolescents to let go in this way. Remember, the adolescent is often having a tough struggle adjusting to the many developmental changes occurring at this time and feeling, or appearing, in any way 'childish' can threaten their sense of accomplishing this task of adaptation. These factors can inhibit the adolescent's grief and mourning, and hence make adapting to the loss more difficult.

Losses in the immediate family are likely to be very traumatic for the adolescent. However, by this stage of development the person is likely to have established significant relationships in the wider family and social group, hence deaths of people beyond the immediate family may also be extremely disturbing. Adolescents often form intense attachments to boyfriends or girlfriends or particular members of their peer group. As we noted in chapter 2 most teenage deaths occur through accidents or suicide. Such losses can shatter an adolescent's sense of identity and confidence, which are often associated with important peer group relationships.

Andy idolised Geoff, who at twenty was three years older than Andy. Geoff was everything Andy wanted to be: he was a musician, he was popular, he had money, girlfriends, his own flat, and a powerful motorcycle. Andy dressed like Geoff and absorbed many of his ideas about life, work and relationships. Without realising it Andy even picked up many of Geoff's mannerisms. Just before his twenty-first birthday, Geoff was killed in a road accident. He had been drinking and was unable to control his motorcycle when a car pulled out quickly from a side-road. Andy was devastated by the loss of someone who had been his idol. He refused to accept that Geoff could have been at fault. While others in his peer group felt sadness at their loss, Andy was consumed with rage. He was unable to talk to anyone about how he felt, and began to vent his anger through frequent arguments and fights, and through drug abuse. Friends who owned motorcycles stopped letting him borrow their vehicles when they realised how reckless his driving had become. Geoff's death seemed to have completely disorientated Andy, whose life became, for a while, chaotic and directionless. Andy's family felt unable to make sense of his behaviour, and did not see the connection between his increasingly disorganised and rebellious actions and the death of his friend. Eventually Andy was able to move beyond his rage to feel his deep sense of sadness and loss. This was accomplished mainly through the support and encouragement of his girlfriend Joanna, who was able to see that Andy's anger and abusive behaviour was an expression of pain and grief. Joanna's recognition and acceptance of Andy's distress eventually helped him to acknowledge and experience his grief, and mourn his loss.

Despite the many factors that make loss during adolescence very difficult to come to terms with, it must again be noted that very often the adolescent's pain and grief are not acknowledged. An adolescent's initial response to a major bereavement will usually be similar to that of an adult: shock, numbness and disbelief. However this is often followed by an attempt to carry on as normal. This strong tendency to suppress feelings of grief is particularly common among male adolescents. But not knowing how to deal with the frightening mix of intense emotions, not knowing how they should respond, how they should behave, are all commonly reported by both male and female adolescents who have suffered a major bereavement. When relationships with the family are strained (which very often occurs for all the reasons noted above) the adolescent simply does not know where to turn for help and guidance.

In this state of confusion and distress many will seek to escape. The complex mix of feelings gets expressed in disguised ways. Within the family the adolescent may appear to continue life as before, or they may complain of minor ills such as headaches, stomach pains or upsets, difficulties eating, insomnia and tiredness. Outside the home the adolescent may engage in what has been termed 'care-eliciting behaviours'. Care-eliciting behaviour refers to any attempt to express and gain recognition for pain and distress in an indirect or covert way. The object may be primarily to receive 'care' (understood very broadly to embrace even the acknowledgement that a person is in distress), but secondary functions include release of tension, perhaps self-punishment, and an attempt to regain the lost person, comparable to the protest phase of attachment behaviour described in chapter 1. Bereaved adolescents may attempt to assuage their distress through sexual relationships which may be engaged in promiscuously and without adequate concern for contraception. The rate of adolescent pregnancies significantly increases following major bereavements. Often, of course, this compounds the difficulty as the adolescent may then suffer another loss through abortion or adoption. Males may engage in more aggressive forms of care-eliciting behaviour. Acts of violence, taking risks, using drugs, various types of 'anti-social' behaviour, self-neglect, challenging authorities, and rejecting the family (the source of the unmanageable pain and grief), appear to be common following bereavement in adolescence. Needless to say much of this behaviour is not recognised for what it is: an attempt both to express and gain recognition for the pain and distress that the adolescent is suffering.

The person engaging in this disguised mourning may actually be quite aware of what they are doing, but more frequently the connections between their loss, their pain, and the care-eliciting behaviours, are not consciously recognised. Often this turmoil is temporary and the adolescent will come to experience and express their grief more directly. Generally for this to happen a place of security or safety is needed, where the adolescent can allow themselves to experience the pain and longing, the helplessness and vulnerability that follows the loss of a loved person. Reports from adolescents in this situation indicate that what is most helpful is openness and honesty. An adult who is not afraid of their own feelings is a valuable model for an adolescent, helping them to accept their feelings without fear, embarrassment or guilt.

During adolescence emotions are usually amplified and an adolescent's love and their hatred will often be extremely intense. Similarly an adolescent's grief can be extremely intense, and mourning can continue in one form or another for many years. Problems can develop when an adolescent has lost a parent and the surviving parents remarries within a year or two of the death. This situation may be particularly difficult for an adolescent because of their tendency to idealise. The dead parent can very easily be seen as ideal and irreplaceable, and anyone moving into their position in the home can be deeply resented. Adolescence is, for many people, a time of rebellion. It is often a particularly difficult time to accept a parent's remarriage, although once again it does appear from research in this area that, despite difficulties, most adolescents are able to mourn their loss and form good relationships with their step-parent.

Loss and the family

The way in which a child responds to loss will be influenced by many factors. The type of relationship that is severed by death, the circumstances of the death, previous experiences of loss, and the patterns of attachment that the child forms are all significant factors contributing to how a child responds to loss. But another crucially important factor is the way in which the child's family, as a system, deals with loss, grief and mourning. The family will usually determine what the child knows about the circumstances of the death, and exert a powerful influence on the type of relationships the child forms. The family will also influence how the child manages strong emotions. In a comprehensive survey of research into bereavement Beverley Raphael, a Professor of Psychiatry in New South Wales, identifies seven distinct patterns of family response to loss, which provides a picture of the varying contexts in which childhood bereavement can occur. The seven patterns of family response are as follows:

The family in which death is taboo
In some families death, grief and mourning are concealed. Children are discouraged from asking questions, and are often 'protected' from grief by being told stories about the dead person being 'on a journey', or having 'gone to be with God'. Children are not allowed to see the body, and are not involved in the funeral. The whole subject of death is avoided. Loss is not talked about, and grief is unacknowledged. Everything to do with death is pushed away, covered with silence. These taboos easily create an atmosphere of dread and fear surrounding death, and grief becomes a very private, even shameful experience. Needless to say such an atmosphere does not help children, or anyone else in the family, deal with their grief and adapt effectively to their loss.

The family in which someone must be to blame
Families in which apportioning blame for the death becomes a major preoccupation, even eclipsing sorrow at the loss, are often very rigid and inflexible in their attitudes to each other and to roles within the family. In family systems such as these a child may associate loss with intense anger and fault-finding. As this inevitably comes to focus on members of the family system itself there is often deep-seated guilt which further disrupts family

relationships. Grief and mourning over loss seems to get displaced by endless debates about who is to blame for the death, or who has failed to act appropriately after the death has occurred. In some cases a vulnerable member of the family, perhaps one of the children, can become a scapegoat for the family's hostility and guilt. It's as if the only time these families can experience a sense of unity and mutual support is when they agree on who to blame. Again, in such an atmosphere it is very difficult for family members to experience their grief and offer each other help and support.

The family in which relationships are avoidant
Raphael describes these families as being built of 'cool' relationships. From early life children are given the message that while relationships are enjoyable and valuable it is unwise to get too close, or invest too much. The assumption of such families is that liking someone too much exposes you to the trauma of loss if the relationship should end, and that such trauma is unmanageable and unbearable. When death strikes, expressions of grief in such families are likely to be short-lived, and adjustment – 'getting on with life' – is likely to be rapid. Children in these families may have to struggle hard to conceal the intensity of their own grief as it will seem to be abnormal, and unacceptable, in a family where people have learnt to remain 'cool' in the face of loss.

The family in which things must go on as before
The changes that naturally follow a major loss are intolerable for some families. The loss may be denied by attempts to fill the gap which it has created by getting another family member to take over the role that has been vacated. Children may be expected to take on a nurturing, comforting role to a parent who has lost their spouse. The family system attempts to minimise the impact of the loss by in some way replacing the person who has died. For this type of denial to work grief must be kept at an absolute minimum, so family members will be discouraged from overt displays of sorrow or mourning.

The family for whom the loss means chaos
Some families already have a fairly precarious sense of unity, with little mutual support. Conflict and divisions are persistent

features of such families. When a death occurs in this context the fragile family system is plunged into chaos. A child in this situation may have to face adapting to the loss of a family member and also the disintegration of the family itself. Support and help from professional agencies may be necessary to help individuals mourn their loss, and to help the family develop a more stable structure despite their bereavement.

The family that must do the right thing
Some families will go to great lengths to ensure that they deal with the death of a family member in 'the right way'. Professionals may be consulted, contacts may be made with voluntary agencies, and books about bereavement read. Advice gained from various sources will be anxiously applied in a concerted effort to make sure the crisis is managed properly. In particular, the parent or parents will be very concerned that the child's needs in this situation are given priority. Raphael notes that while such families may cope with a major loss 'reasonably well', the family system is attempting to manage and control feelings through a predominantly rational or intellectual approach. Children in these families, though benefiting from being involved in funeral arrangements, perhaps seeing the body of the deceased, and receiving careful and honest explanations of what is happening, may also sense that the feelings associated with death and mourning are fearful and traumatic experiences that must be defended against. The disturbing reality of loss and the pain of grief can appear to be stifled beneath an earnest effort to get the arrangements and practical details 'right'.

The family that functions with openness and sharing of feelings
According to Raphael, the family system that is most helpful for children suffering bereavement is one in which the various relationships in the family are characterised by a readiness to express and accept a range of feelings, both positive and negative, without fear of recrimination. Although these families experience loss acutely there is a high level of shared grief and mutual support and comfort. The disturbance often associated with mourning is accepted within the family without fear, shame or guilt. A child experiencing bereavement in this family

context learns that although loss is painful the feelings are not unmanageable or unacceptable. The child also learns that the complex experiences of grief and mourning can be shared with others, and further, that healing can come through such sharing.

Summary

In this chapter we have noted that at different stages of childhood and adolescence there are specific factors that add to the difficulties of coming to terms with a major bereavement. We have also noted that grief and mourning in children and adolescents often goes unacknowledged. Sensitivity to the special difficulties young people face when trying to cope with a major loss requires openness, honesty and a willingness to share the difficulties and pain of grief and mourning.

4 Grief and mourning in adult life

As an individual grows and matures new relationships are formed and older ones may be lost. Deaths are likely to occur across a wide network of relationships. Bereavements may be experienced within the immediate family of origin (parents, brothers and sisters) and the wider family (for example, grandparents, aunts and uncles). But death may also claim friends and acquaintances, colleagues and associates. The central feature of most people's adult life is the establishment of a stable sexual relationship, and, for many, having children of their own. The intimate bond, or attachment, between sexual partners is often the source of the greatest satisfaction in life, and perhaps at times the greatest distress. The love experienced between sexual partners – heterosexual or homosexual – brings not only great fulfilment, but also carries the unavoidable risk that if the bond is broken intense emotional pain will result. For some this risk may be too difficult to bear, they may resist love and intimacy and remain emotionally detached in their relationships. The bonds of love established between parents and their children are also often both enduring and intense. In early life the child's attachment to his or her primary care-giver is a matter of life and death, and parents usually respond by placing children at the centre of their life. For many adults the death of their partner, or the death of a son or daughter, constitutes their worst nightmare.

In the course of adult life we are likely to experience various losses, within the family and in the wider social network. Where the attachment to the person who has died was strong and close, the pain of grief is likely to be intense. As noted in chapters 1 and 3, bereavements in early life can exert a powerful influence on the formation of later relationships, and the way in which adults respond to loss in later life. Bereavement in adult life seems to revive experiences of early losses. This is especially so when the loss involves the severing of a strong attachment. So for an adult the type of attachment and the past history of loss will be very significant factors influencing how that adult responds to loss. Another crucial factor is the way in which the loss has occurred. About 50% of all deaths occur suddenly. Sudden deaths leave no opportunity for preparation, for what is sometimes called 'anticipatory grief', which appears to help the mourning process after the death. Where the death is both sudden and violent (perhaps through suicide, murder, or an accident) the loss is likely to be particularly difficult to come to terms with.

Another factor contributing to the adult's experience of loss concerns the different ways that men and women deal with grief. In general greater allowances are made for women to express grief than for men. Our society is both more tolerant of, and more sympathetic to, the overt display of grief in women, and uncomfortable with expressions of grief in men. Many of the aspects of grief described in chapter 1 can result in the bereaved person feeling weak and helpless. Many bereaved people find themselves feeling and behaving in ways reminiscent of childhood – for example, wanting to be held or comforted, being unable to care for themselves properly, and feeling frightened and insecure. Men may find these feelings particularly distressing and undermining. They contradict many of the stereotypes of what it is to be male in our society and hence may be a source of shame. Men many also find it difficult to ask for help, or express their feelings to other family members or friends. Some may try to 'put on a brave face' and attempt to continue to cope without help from others. This attempt to bear the pain of loss alone merely adds to the burden of grief, and deprives the mourners of valuable social support. Expressing feelings, perhaps asking for help explicitly, may not come easily, but without such behaviours other people may hold back, not wanting to intrude. British society does not encourage overt displays of emotion, and strongly discourages what can be perceived as weakness. We are expected to carry on regardless. As noted in chapter 2 the type of society in which someone has been brought up profoundly influences their experience of loss; sometimes society helps the process of mourning, at other times it can add to the difficulties. Unfortunately British reserve, distance, and lack of emotional expression, can often be a serious obstacle in the path of bereaved people trying to adapt to loss.

In adult life there are two types of loss that most people

dread, and that are likely to be particularly traumatic. These are the death of a sexual partner, and the death of a child. In this chapter we will focus on these two major bereavements in the first two sections, and consider other forms of adult bereavement in the third section.

Death of a partner

Intimate relationships vary. Some relationships are all-embracing, one or both partners deriving all or most of their satisfactions from just the one intimate relationship. People 'put into' and 'get out of' their relationships very different things. Some relationships are balanced and reciprocal. Others are 'one-sided'. Levels of dependence and independence vary. Such factors may be stable or they may change over time. Our sense of identity, our sense of personal worth, even what we consider to be our purpose in life, may largely be based on our relationship with our partner. Of course people vary in the extent to which this is true: people, and the relationships they form, are very complex and highly varied. But the point to note is that the impact of losing a partner is closely related to what the relationship meant to the survivor. When we say of someone that they 'mean a lot' to us, we are not just talking about our feelings for them. As we noted in chapter 1 other people can be of enormous significance to us, even to the extent of forming aspects of our identity. The significance of the relationship, what it meant to us, will profoundly affect the way we respond to the loss of the relationship.

When a partner dies it can take many months for the survivor to realise how much has been lost. Sally and Katherine had lived together for fifteen years. Katherine died suddenly from a brain haemorrhage when she was forty. A year after the death Sally described her loss as follows:

> Katherine was always there, always so reliable, I just didn't realise how much of my life centred on her. Since her death it feels I have had to experience over and over again a sense of being broken apart. Every time I turn to say something to her the realisation that she's gone is like another break in my world. Bit by bit I've had to realise how much Katherine meant to me: as a lover, as a comforter, as the

level-headed one who took care of the bills, as the only person who seemed to understand my sense of humour, as the person who nursed me when I was ill, and who listened to my complaints about life, as the person who I was able to help and support when she felt low, as the person who wanted and needed me, and many, many more losses that took months to realise. I was left not knowing what to do, or even who I was.

Sally's experience reveals the extent to which losing a partner can affect the survivor's sense of identity.

We have noted that a factor that can make loss particularly difficult is when the bereaved person has strong but mixed feelings about the deceased. Some level of ambivalence is bound to be present in any close relationship, and is something all close relationships must come to terms with. With the death of a loved partner ambivalent feelings can surface with distressing intensity. This was expressed very clearly by Paul, whose wife Nicola died in her early thirties in a road accident, leaving two children, Donna and Sue.

At first I just couldn't believe it. When I realised it was true, she wouldn't be coming home, I didn't know how I would cope. I kept hearing her voice, telling me to be strong for the children, asking me if the children were all right. This went on for months. I put all my energy into providing for Donna and Sue. Looking back it's like I was in a dream; working, housework, caring for the children. Then after two years I suddenly woke up: 'What about me?' It was then that I started to feel resentment: Why did she go? Why wasn't she more careful? I remembered Nicola had often said 'you'll be sorry when I'm gone' after we had rowed about something. It sounds crazy now, but I felt so angry, she seemed to have left us deliberately. But how can you have such feelings for someone you love?

When the loss is sudden, and particularly for those in Paul's situation where the partner is young, it may take some time for the reality of the loss to 'sink in'. The survivor may expect the deceased will return at any moment, the whole thing having been a mistake. But as the truth is progressively accepted, powerful feelings related to the loss usually surface. Some of these feelings may be very difficult to acknowledge, and very difficult to express. As the survivor thinks through the events surrounding the death they may experience intense regret about something they did, or did not do. 'If only...' is a common thought – the survivor wishing they had done something to avert the death. This can easily lead to self criticism and blame 'I should have phoned the doctor sooner', 'I wish I had never bought the car', 'I should have realised something was wrong'. Criticism and blame may also be directed at others – it may be felt that relatives should have been more helpful, or the doctor should have been more skilled. Sometimes this can be a way of expressing anger towards the deceased in an indirect way because the anger is simply too painful to acknowledge directly.

Regret and self-criticism may also occur when the survivor thinks back through the relationship. This 'relationship review' is an important part of the process of mourning. As noted in chapter 1 the survivor will try to find a place for the deceased in their affections and their memory. Reviewing the past is crucial to this process, and often needs to be done repeatedly. The survivor may do this privately, not being able to think of anything else; or he or she may talk to others. Although it may be painful and difficult to hear what the survivor wants, and needs, to express, simply listening – without offering advice, trying to change the subject, or make them feel better – is extremely valuable for the bereaved person.

The bereaved partner will usually be thought of as the 'prime griever', or 'prime mourner'. But the death may reverberate through many levels of family and friends. The bereaved partner must manage the changed relationships brought about by the loss as well as their own grief. Where there are children, especially if they are young, there will be intense pressure for the bereaved partner to 'be strong for the sake of the children'. This is particularly so for men. This is a complex situation in which each family member has lost a central figure in their life, but the deceased will have had a unique significance to each member. No individual's loss is the same as another. For example, a teenage girl's relationship to her father is very different to the relationship between her father and her five-year-old brother. Each loss is unique, each person's pain is individual and special. As each loss is unique, the needs of each of the bereaved family members will be different. Similarly the process of mourning and the expression of grief are likely to be different for each member. This can be both confusing and upsetting for all those involved. A bereaved partner has to struggle with the very considerable burden of dealing with their own major loss, and responding to the individual needs of the bereaved children. This is clearly one of the most demanding and one of the most painful situations that an adult can be confronted with.

A situation can arise in which there is competition for the role of 'prime griever'. Perhaps the deceased had a particularly close relationship with a parent, who feels that no-one could experience the loss as intensely as they do. This can occur in particular where the parents have not accepted the relationship that their son or daughter had formed. Phillip and Eve had never accepted their son David's homosexuality and had opposed his relationship with Michael. Although David and Michael had established a close stable bond, a deeply satisfying relationship in which both felt secure and happy, Phillip and Eve simply could not accept the situation. When David died in a road traffic accident, Eve saw herself as the 'prime mourner' and wanted to organise funeral arrangements. She could not bring herself to see the love Michael felt for David – or the intensity of his grief. The emotional turmoil associated with such conflicts are not easily managed, and in some cases can seriously disrupt the process of mourning.

In chapter 1 we reviewed the description of the Four Tasks of Mourning given by William Worden. The Fourth Task was: To Emotionally Relocate the Deceased and Move on With Life. 'Moving on with life' often involves the formation of a new relationship, and may present numerous difficulties. The formation of a new sexual relationship may be inhibited by a sense of loyalty to the deceased partner. The survivor may feel they would be betraying their partner if they entered into another relationship. This feeling would suggest that the process of separating and severing the attachment (finding a place for the deceased inwardly) requires more time. Well-meaning relatives and friends (and perhaps some less well-meaning) may encourage the bereaved person to form a new intimate attachment as soon as possible. This is unlikely to be helpful. Children may find it very difficult to adjust to a new 'mother' or 'father', and may find it difficult to understand the parent's needs in this matter.

Motives for forming a new relationship vary. Some may simply want the contact with another person in order to be comforted. Frequently this will only be available as part of a sexual encounter. The sexual needs and feelings of bereaved people is a subject that is often ignored. Evidence suggests wide variation: some bereaved people describe sharp increases in sexual desire after loss of their partner, while others lose all interest in sex. These individual differences are part of the wide range of 'normal' responses to loss. The need to be held and comforted is very common, and perfectly natural, but it is a desire that may be unacknowledged. The bereaved adult may feel compelled to seek sexual contact as a way of receiving physical comfort, even if desire for sexual intercourse is minimal. A bereaved person in this position is vulnerable and there is a risk of entering into relationships that are less than helpful. Essentially, physical contact is being sought as a means of reducing the pain of loss. A relationship formed on this basis may provide short-term comfort but it would be unwise to assume this is evidence of long-term compatibility.

Death of a child

Parents can be bereaved in various ways. The loss may be due to miscarriage or abortion, stillbirth, neonatal death or 'sudden infant death syndrome' (SIDS). Such losses are not infrequent; in fact in Britain one in four confirmed pregnancies end in loss. Later losses during childhood or adolescence are much less common, being comparatively rare events. Each of these situations involves problems specific to the particular type of death. In this section we will consider each situation in turn.

What has been said in the previous section about bereavement being, in some sense, a loss of part of the self is often experienced acutely when an adult faces the death of a child. Parental attachment to a child begins at conception. This is especially true for the mother. A pregnant woman and her developing baby are literally attached, connected physically, to the extent of forming a single system. Her baby is part of her; there is literally no space between them. The process of birth and growth through infancy to adulthood involves progressive separation and distance between the child and his or her mother. At various points in this process the mother may experience the child's growth as her loss. As a child becomes more independent the mother may feel her role diminishes in importance. A growing child can mean a loss of valued roles, and severe disruption of identity for some mothers. This sense of loss can in turn lead to feelings of resentment which are, of course, difficult to harmonise with the nonetheless genuine feelings of love. Although the development and growing independence of a child can be experienced, particularly by the child's mother, as a distressing loss, if the child should actually die these feelings are often greatly amplified.

In 'developed' societies most deaths of children result from accidents; comparatively few are the result of illness. In the case of sudden death there is no opportunity for anticipating grief – no opportunity to prepare for the loss. As most parents who lose a child will do so through an accident, most will have to face this ordeal without time to prepare themselves for the loss. But one situation where the loss is anticipated is abortion.

Evidence suggests women react to abortions in very different ways. Some women appear to be only marginally affected by it. For others termination is a significant loss which leads to intense grief and prolonged mourning. Abortion involves a decision, a choice, which may require denying grief in order to carry it through.

Meg was sixteen when she had an abortion. Her mother and father insisted it was the 'right thing to do', and that she should put it behind her, focus on passing exams and getting to university. Her boyfriend, Ben, had a place at university and, although he was very fond of Meg, did not want to commit himself to a long-term relationship. Ben reassured Meg that her parents were right. Meg was determined to go to university; she felt her brother and sister had missed out, in terms of opportunities and experiences, by marrying young and starting families early. Meg also knew that her relationship with Ben would not survive indefinitely. As she said, 'common sense', her rational side, told her to terminate the pregnancy. But somehow her feelings, her emotions and her body, did not agree. After the abortion she found it impossible to concentrate on her studies, and would frequently burst into tears 'for no reason'. Meg tried desperately to hide these feelings from others, and feared that she was 'having a nervous breakdown'.

The circumstances surrounding Meg's decision to terminate her pregnancy are crucial. There was very little recognition of her mixed feelings about the pregnancy. Her family and boy-friend expected her to be pleased and relieved that it was over. To some extent she did experience these feelings. But she also felt grief. Her experience was not recognised as a loss for her. No one seemed to recognise that her abortion was a bereavement. She was expected to feel relief not sorrow. Her grief was not understood by those close to her, but she was also intolerant of these feelings herself. Meg protested against the way she felt: 'Why do I feel like this? I made the choice, and I wouldn't change it. I should be happy, why do I feel so bad?' Feelings are rarely straightforward. The difficulty in understanding Meg's situation arises when we fail to recognise that it is possible, and in fact is remarkably common, to experience opposite or conflicting feelings about the same situation or towards the same person. Meg's parents felt she should be relieved that an abortion is so simple and safe. It seemed the most obvious, most straightforward way of dealing with the situation. This view fails to take account of the complexity of human emotions. Meg both wanted to be free of responsibility in order to go to university, and at the same time longed to be a mother. Furthermore, she had anxieties about the consequences of the abortion. Would she be harmed? Would her next pregnancy be all right? Would she be punished? What would her future husband think of her actions? All the people closely involved in this situation – including Meg herself – were trying to avoid looking at these questions and the difficult feelings underlying them. The situation was in fact very much more complicated than it at first appeared, and indeed much more complicated than those involved wished it to be.

Meg's experience illustrates a point that has been emphasised in earlier chapters: much grief in our society goes unrecognised. We seem so preoccupied with how and what people 'should' or 'shouldn't' feel that we fail to recognise what people – ourselves and others – do in fact feel. This failure of recognition adds immeasurably to the difficulties of adapting to loss.

A woman can choose to have an abortion, but pregnancy may also end through miscarriage, or result in stillbirth, or the infant may die very soon after the birth. In each of these situations the months of pregnancy are likely to have been full of anticipation and preparation for the birth. Some would argue that the process of building attachment and bonding to the child would have begun from the time the mother knew she was pregnant. Where an abortion has been chosen the connection or attachment is severed involuntarily. In these other situations – miscarriage, stillbirth and neonatal death – the attachment is severed unwillingly.

One central difficulty in these situations is that the parents' preparations for the baby may have been very extensive – emotionally and materially. Returning home without the expected baby can be very traumatic. Once again we can note that grief in this situation may not be acknowledged. In particular the father's grief may be unrecognised by others and perhaps by the father himself. But it should also be remembered that other family members also suffer the bereavement – for example, brothers and sisters expecting a new sibling, and grandparents looking forward to a grandchild. Many parents in this situation experience considerable guilt – feeling that somehow they caused the death, either by something they failed to do, or through have produced a 'defective' infant. There may also be awareness of having mixed feelings about the baby; perhaps abortion was considered, or one or both parents felt unsure about having the child. It is also not uncommon for couples to blame each other for the death. In such situations finding a cause, a reason for the death, may be desperately pursued as a way of making sense of the tragedy. Couples may become angry at each other, or the hospital, or even other family members who may not have been as helpful or supportive as they could have been, or perhaps were negative in some way about the birth. Such anger is not an unusual response in these circumstances. A further source of conflict concerns the way men and women respond to loss. A father's grief may be much less visible, and he may even appear cold and detached. Family and friends may tend to withdraw, not knowing what to say, or how best to respond to the couple's difficulties. Other children may also be confused, frightened, and perhaps angry at what is happening in the family, especially if their own envy of the new child had been significant. All of these factors contribute to the difficulties of coming to terms with the loss of the child and, needless to say, can be a tremendous strain on the couple's relationship.

Janet gave birth to her stillborn son, Sean, after being rushed to hospital in the eighth month of her pregnancy. Sean was the third of three sons. This is the type of situation that can be handled very poorly, but Janet was fortunate in that hospital staff were aware of the importance of recognising that, despite being stillborn, Sean was Janet's child. She had given birth to a son, and she would need to grieve and mourn his death. Janet was allowed to hold her son on several occasions during the day following the birth. Her partner, Malcolm, was able to take a photograph of Janet holding Sean, and a nurse took a photograph of the whole family: Janet, Malcolm, Sean and his two brothers. Sean was part of a family and each member of the family would mourn their loss. Despite her grief Janet felt her loss was made easier to bear by the hospital staff.

> Of course I was upset, but seeing and holding Sean and having the photographs to keep made me feel that the pregnancy and birth were real, and that Sean was real. He was part of our family. I've read of other women who don't see their stillborn son or daughter, they're left with nothing – as if the pregnancy and all the plans were just dreams, something to be embarrassed and guilty about. The hospital helped with the funeral, without taking it over. I think that's important. We wanted to say goodbye to Sean, he was our son, he had been with us for eight months, and we loved him. Of course I felt terrible when I saw pregnant mums, or mothers with newborn babies. But thank God no one said, 'Don't worry, you've got two other sons', 'you can always try again'. Sean was our third child, he was an individual, a person. Losing him was painful, he was our son, that can't be taken from us, he wasn't something just to be got rid of and be embarrassed about.

Janet expresses very clearly the point that, despite the pain of such losses, the experience can be made easier to bear by the sensitive response of hospital staff. Of course it does not follow from experiences like Janet's that it is always helpful for the mother to see and hold her stillborn baby. In some situations it may be unwise. The Stillbirth and Neonatal Death Society (SANDS) has conducted a national survey that demonstrates wide variations in how different hospitals deal with stillborn and neonatal deaths. Two major questions investigated in the survey concern whether the mother and father should be allowed to see their dead infant, and what should be done with the infant's body. While some hospitals are aware of the delicacy of these issues and deal with them very sensitively, unfortunately this is not the case in all hospitals. The SANDS report stresses the importance of parental choice in these matters and the need for hospital staff to consult parents, rather than making decisions for them. It appears from such studies that there is a need for greater awareness of the fact that stillbirths and neonatal deaths are bereavements that parents and other family members naturally respond to with grief and mourning. Furthermore, if it is the parents' choice, it is entirely appropriate that a funeral service be arranged, as with any other bereavement. Such recognition can help parents adapt to their loss without having to suffer the additional burdens of shame and guilt.

Among older children deaths occur most frequently through accidents. As noted in chapter 1 there are usually strong bonds of attachment between the young child and, in particular, his or her mother. These are particularly intense during the early years of infancy. As a child grows and seeks more independence it is common for parents to experience more negative feelings towards the child. There may be resentment about the loss of exclusive attachment; a sense of having to 'stand back' and allow the child to grow and change may be difficult to bear. Difficulties adjusting to the child's growth may reflect the parents' own early attachment experiences. If this is so the feelings involved may be very difficult to understand, and perhaps at times seem overwhelming. This sense of gradually losing the child as he or she grows can be very painful. This pain may be difficult to acknowledge and be hidden, or defended against by being angry with the child or rejecting him or her. Thoughts or fantasies which may involve wishing the child was not there, or wishing they were young, 'cuddly' and dependent again, may be a source of intense guilt if the child should become seriously ill, or be involved in an accident. These difficult feelings are often at their most intense when the child has reached adolescence. During adolescence there is often conflict in the family, with testing of boundaries and rebelliousness in one form or another. The turmoil of adolescence may involve various risk-taking activities, such as the use of illegal drugs, or reckless driving. The changes experienced during adolescence also often involve significant emotional upheaval. 'Falling in love', infatuations of various sorts, and difficulties in developing a sense of independent identity, can be very distressing both for the adolescent and for his or her parents. We have noted that the suicide rate among adolescents is high. Parents who lose a son or daughter through suicide may well have had to deal with considerable conflict prior to the death, and feel guilt and remorse for this after the suicide.

Carlton committed suicide at the age of eighteen. His parents, Valerie and Stuart, described their hopes for him in his early years. The family were devoted churchgoers and Carlton had shown such enthusiasm for Christianity that Valerie and Stuart had hoped he would eventually train for the priesthood. However, when he was fifteen Carlton's interest in religion appeared to wane. He became absorbed in music and formed a rock band with some friends. His behaviour became progressively more distressing to his parents: staying out until the early hours of the morning, coming home drunk, doing very poorly in school exams. Although Valerie and Stuart attempted to impose limits on his behaviour their efforts seemed to provoke greater rebelliousness. Bitter arguments became a daily occurrence. Eventually, after leaving school, Carlton left home and lived with various friends over the following two years. During this period Valerie and Stuart saw him very rarely, in fact only when he came to their home to borrow money, which was never returned. After two years away from home Carlton asked his parents if he could move back with them for a while as he was now homeless. Carlton appeared desperate and so Valerie and Stuart allowed him to return on condition he conduct himself with more respect than had previously been the case. Carlton assured them he would, but soon after his return conflicts developed once again. Carlton spent most of his time sleeping and was withdrawn and uncommunicative. At night he would insist on playing music which, as they lived in a flat, led to complaints from various neighbours.

Valerie and Stuart tried everything to change Carlton's behaviour. They asked members of the church to call to see him in an attempt to rekindle his interest in Christianity. When this failed they tried threats. But the situation continued to deteriorate, the arguments becoming more aggressive. Valerie and Stuart were convinced Carlton was taking drugs, and they threatened to call the police. Early one morning Carlton took his life by jumping from the balcony of the flat. Valerie and Stuart were deeply shocked by their son's suicide. They had to struggle with the loss of a greatly loved only child who had been the focus of their lives for many years, and the painful awareness of the high levels of conflict and ill feeling that had characterised the relationship for the previous few years. Stuart recalled how he had shouted at Carlton, saying his behaviour was killing his mother, and that it would have been better if he had never been born. In such circumstances the pain of grief is exacerbated by the memory of conflict and ill feeling, and such losses are certainly among the most difficult to come to terms with.

Other bereavements in adult life

The loss of a partner and the loss of a child are situations that most people will readily recognise as major personal crises. This recognition from others helps legitimise grief and mourning and makes it more likely that help and support will be available. However, there are other losses in adult life that often receive little recognition. Among these are the loss of elderly parents, the loss of grandparents, the loss of grandchildren, and the loss of friends. In these situations it may be expected that the grief should be relatively manageable and adaptation to the loss relatively quick. The significance of a relationship, and hence the impact of the loss, may not be appreciated by family members, friends and neighbours, because of assumptions about what people 'should' feel in relation to particular losses. But once again we need to bear in mind the fact that there are no 'rules' of mourning. There is a wide range of individual differences in response to loss.

Jack and Ken had been friends for over thirty years. In their younger years they were inseparable. As Jack put it, they 'had helped each other out of trouble and fought each other's battles'. Both had had periods of unemployment, and both had experienced periods of relative wealth. Each had been 'best man' at the other's wedding, and they had managed to maintain a close friendship despite both raising families. Jack and Paula had had four children, Ken and Maureen had had three. Although both families had spent a great deal of time together, going on holidays and even at one time sharing a house, everyone seemed to understand that the real bond was between Jack and Ken. Jack had been an only child, and Ken had had four sisters but no brothers. 'We were like brothers, me and Ken. Neither of us had a brother at home so I think we made up for that by treating each other as a brother'. Ken died in his late forties of lung cancer. His wife and family were devastated by the loss, and Jack saw it as his responsibility to help them cope with the changes brought by the loss. For months after Ken's death Jack was busy doing all that he could for Ken's family.

> Keeping busy stopped me from realising what had happened. I just kept thinking 'what would Ken want me to do?'. The answer was obvious: 'Help Maureen and the family'. So that's what I did. But seven or eight months after Ken died I started getting panicky feelings. Out of the blue I would start sweating, and my heart would start thumping. This went on for months. Then I started imagining I could see Ken in the street. Out of the corner of my eye, I would think it was him, then I would look and realise it was a mistake. As the months passed this got worse. About a year after Ken's death I decided to visit his grave on my own. That's when it really hit me. I had finally stopped rushing around and realised Ken was dead. I stood there in the cemetery, in the pouring rain, sobbing like a child. I just couldn't stop, the tears were flooding out of me. And the worst thing about it was I felt ashamed. You hear about people losing their wife, or their kid dies, and they crack up from it. But here's me, a fifty-year-old man with a great wife and family, falling to pieces when a mate dies. Who's going to understand that?

Frank had worked hard to establish himself in the highly competitive world of insurance. He felt that life had offered him few opportunities, but what opportunities he did have he had exerted himself to make the most of. He had a reputation for discipline, tough-mindedness and, as he acknowledged himself, 'a certain ruthlessness'.

Frank was the eldest of three children; he was four years old when his father left, and five when his mother's new partner moved in. Over the next few years Frank spent more and more time at his grandmother's house because he had quickly come to 'hate' his mother's new partner. Eventually Frank moved into his grandmother's permanently, partly because he felt 'squeezed out' by the birth of two more children, but also because he felt much more 'at home' with his grandmother. When he was ten years old Frank's mother and family moved to another city. After this contact virtually ceased. Frank's hatred for his stepfather was matched by his devotion to his grandmother. His hard work and material success had been in some sense for her; a way of showing that her care for him had not been misplaced. Frank's grandmother died in her mid-eighties after a brief illness. Frank was completely unprepared for the impact of her death. He knew, of course, that he would be upset but the intensity of his feelings, and the extent to which his grief disrupted his life, came as a profound shock to him. There was no-one in Frank's life who he felt would be able to understand his experience. His view of himself, as someone in a responsible and demanding position, used to taking hard and often unpopular decisions and able to bear prolonged stress and uncertainty, simply did not allow for the depth of feeling and vulnerability that seemed to explode into his life when his grandmother died. To make sense of these feelings Frank needed time to allow himself to realise what his relationship with his grandmother had meant to him. His feelings made sense in the light of the significance of his loss. In order to allow him to mourn his loss he needed to put aside some of his stereotypes about what someone in his position should and should not feel about the death of an elderly relative. Both Frank and his relationship to his grandmother were unique and, as he eventually saw, the extent of his grief both understandable and healthy.

Summary

We have noted that major losses in adult life – the death of a partner, or child, or other significant relationship – are in themselves traumatic enough but may be made more difficult when the loss is not fully recognised. Adult grief is complex and varied, and individuals will respond to loss in unique ways. The circumstances surrounding the loss, and the way others respond to the bereaved person, can exert a dramatic influence on the experience of grief and mourning.

5 Anticipatory grief and mourning

About 50% of deaths in Britain occur suddenly, without warning. In the other 50% there is at least some expectation that the death will occur, or is likely to occur. As noted in chapter 2 sudden deaths, especially those involving violence, are often particularly difficult to come to terms with. In contrast there is evidence that, for some, adapting to loss may be helped when the loss is expected. The period prior to the death can be a valuable opportunity to prepare for the loss; that is, the difficult process of adapting to the loss of a loved one can begin before the death occurs. When this happens the experience is often termed 'anticipatory grief and mourning'. In this chapter we will consider some of the more important aspects of preparing for loss. Much of the material in this chapter focuses on what is probably the main issue in effective anticipatory mourning, that of communication between the dying person and those who will mourn their loss.

Preparing for loss: hope and consummation

Preparing for loss – anticipatory grief and mourning – involves experiencing many of the features of grief and mourning described in the early pages of this book. An initial period of numbness, followed perhaps by anger or blame (especially of hospital authorities), may then give way to fear, desperation and perhaps despair. The anticipation of loss provokes many of the same responses as an actual loss. But the important difference is, of course, that the period of grief and mourning has begun before the death has occurred, and while contact and communication with the dying person is still possible. Because of this fact the period before the death can be a time of hope as well as grief, a time of opportunity as well as sorrow.

During the period of anticipation, when a death is expected and doctors have 'done all they can', family and friends may feel that 'there is no hope', there is nothing that can be done. But this is certainly not the case. Hope can take many forms. When the hope of cure, the hope that death may be averted, is given up, that does not mean there is no hope left. Anticipatory grief and mourning may involve deep sadness but need not be without hope. Hope can mean many things. The obvious ones are cure, or some form of afterlife. But there are many other hopes. Hope that the loved person dies with a minimum of pain, with as much comfort and dignity as possible, having healed any rifts in close relationships, having attained a sense of peace and acceptance, and that they do not die alone or plagued by regrets, are all legitimate hopes that often form part of anticipatory mourning. For those with religious or spiritual commitments and beliefs hope may concern other aspects of the manner of dying, and expectations of an afterlife. And, of course, one does not need to be religious in the formal sense to see that, as Sherwin Nuland puts it: 'the promise of spiritual companionship near the end' is also a source of hope.

So the period of anticipation prior to the death of a loved person can be one of hope as well as grief. Although anticipatory mourning can involve various hopes for the dying person, an important aspect of hope concerns both the dying person and the mourners themselves. This is the hope that the dying person and those close to them will be able to achieve some sort of 'final consummation' in their relationships. 'Consummation' means 'completion' or 'fulfilment', it contains the idea of achieving an end that is in some way a natural unfolding of what is already present. Consummation may involve the 'healing' (or making 'whole') of a relationship that has been damaged. Consummation in this context would include freeing the relationship of obstacles, of old resentments and grudges, and affirming what had been at the heart of the relationship – the love that may have been eclipsed but now needs to be affirmed. Regrets for things not said or done, affection not expressed, or forgiveness withheld, can greatly add to the burden of loss. How often bereaved people recall experiencing an impulse to hug the dying person or tell them they love them but held back. 'If only...' is unfortunately very commonly heard after a death has occurred and the opportunity lost. Regrets about what has or has not been said or done is often referred to as 'unfinished business'. This is not a good term – relationships are not about 'doing business' – but it does at least capture the notion of something that has not been carried through to its natural end, that is incomplete. The period prior to the death of a loved person doubtlessly involves pain and sorrow, but can also be a valuable time for communication, affection, intimacy, care, support, sharing what is happening and what has passed, and attaining some sense of completion or consummation in the relationship. It seems that where this is possible the memories of such consummation appear to help the process of adapting to the loss after the death has occurred. In fact, such experiences can contribute to what Stephen Levine, in his book *Who Dies?*, has called 'the transformation of tragedy into grace'.

Should the dying person be told?

When someone is dying the next of kin will often be informed as a matter of routine. The question of whether to inform the person facing death is not an easy one to answer. Surveys suggest a majority of doctors (80% of those questioned) felt it unhelpful to let someone know they are dying. But studies have shown between 50% and 80% of patients want to know the truth. It seems that most relatives are also unwilling to let a loved one be told that they are dying. It is important to understand why there is often a reluctance to tell patients directly that they are dying. There are three general reasons offered in support of this reluctance.

Firstly, you can never be one hundred per cent certain that the illness the patient is suffering from will lead to their death. Spontaneous remission (an unpredictable reversal of the disease process leading to recovery) does occur, even in situations where the disease has become considerably advanced. Although such spontaneous cures are rare, it may be argued that you can never be absolutely sure it would not happen in any particular case. Secondly, hope is an important part of recovery from any illness. When someone gives up hope their capacity to fight the disease seems to be impaired. Maintaining hope and the 'will to live' may extend life, or at least improve the quality of the life that remains. Thirdly, telling someone they are dying is likely to provoke disturbing feelings of anxiety, perhaps even panic, sadness and depression, and often anger. (Apart from these reasons, which appear to reflect concern for the welfare of the patient, there may of course be other motives for withholding the truth. It may be that health care workers have difficulty accepting death because they associate death with their own professional failure. It may be easier to collude in a denial of death than accept feelings of professional inadequacy.)

Reflecting on these three factors many health care workers feel that in most cases it would be unwise to tell someone that they are dying. But these three arguments need to be compared with the arguments offered in support of the alternative view. Firstly, as noted above, many patients say they want to know the truth. It is further suggested that while health care workers may be better informed than a patient regarding the best way to treat an illness, it does not follow from this that the professional knows in all respects what is best for the patient. Secondly, it is very often the case that the dying person knows the truth, but colludes with the pretence and avoidance of staff and relatives because they do not want to cause a disturbance, or upset people. This may seem strange, but many researchers in the field have reported the dying person's concern for others as being a prime reason for going along with a pretence that they will recover, or be able to return home, or should make plans for the future. As noted above, it may be that the refusal to discuss openly the subject of a patient's death may be more to do with protecting the feelings of professionals than with the care of the dying. Thirdly, maintaining a pretence and avoiding the truth takes away the opportunity for sharing and experiencing some sort of consummation as described in the previous section. The concern that bringing the truth out into the open risks the patient and the relatives being overwhelmed by their feelings is certainly understandable. But this risk needs to be set against the benefits of open communication between the dying person and those close to them. Even in a family where feelings have not been expressed freely the opportunity to say goodbye in a meaningful way may be considerably less stressful than maintaining a pretence – for both patient and relatives. Although it may seem cold or even morbid to do so, it is also an opportunity to discuss matters that the dying person will leave behind. To discuss the practical issues of setting affairs in order, finances, insurance, making a will, funeral arrangements, and other matters, may be extremely helpful for both parties. Such practical issues can cause immense stress to mourners when there is uncertainty or conflict, and can be more easily resolved if there is an opportunity to discuss them with the dying person. Communication between the dying person and those close to them can be invaluable in preventing difficulties after the death has occurred. We have noted how often mourners experience regret for things not said, or things left undone, how often bereaved people say 'If only...'. Where there is time to prepare for a death there is opportunity to deal with these matters.

Among those who advocate telling patients the truth about their prognosis there is a keen awareness that the manner in which the truth is presented will have a significant influence on the way it is received. The main question is not *whether* a dying person should be told the truth, but rather *how* and *when* it should be done.

A situation may arise in which you, as the next of kin, are informed that someone you love is dying. Hospital staff may recommend you do not tell the patient the truth. Perhaps they will suggest this and offer reasons similar to those outlined above. This, of course, places you in a very difficult position. The final decision rests with you. You may choose to act against the recommendations of the medical staff and speak openly to your loved one about the diagnosis and their approaching death. This is not an easy decision to make. Those who recommend protecting the patient may offer very reasonable argument to support their view, and these should be taken into account. Discussing your concerns with hospital staff and with other relatives may clarify the advantages and disadvantages of the opposing views. But after considering the different sides it is you who must make the final decision.

If you decide to talk openly with your loved one there are some general guidelines that can make the process easier. The first principle is to allow the dying person to say how serious the problem is. It is important to remember that in many cases patients are aware that they are dying but hold back from saying anything. It is helpful to let them know that you are willing to talk openly. Give the person a chance to express what they have been thinking or feeling. This can be done with a simple question such as: 'How serious do you think it is?', or, 'What do you feel is going to happen?' A second key principle is to move gradually towards the truth. It is certainly not advisable to tell someone in an abrupt way that they are going to die. A gradual approach to the truth can involve saying something about the current position with their medical treatment: 'The doctors have tried their best. It seems the most they can offer now is to make you as comfortable as possible'. Dealing with such delicate matters is not easy. Care and sensitivity regarding the timing and manner of communicating the truth are essential.

People facing their own death can react in very different ways. But despite the differences in response it is possible to describe certain common reactions. It is very helpful to be aware of these reactions as they will help us to understand what sort of difficulties are likely to arise when communicating with someone who is dying. We will consider these two issues in the next two sections.

The experience of dying

When a person is told that they are dying, they appear to experience what can be termed 'anticipatory grief and mourning' for the loss of their own life, and everything that they have valued in their life. The experience of dying, the complex pattern of responses that facing one's own death provokes, has been documented in great detail in recent years. But a landmark in our understanding of this field is the early work of Elizabeth Kübler-Ross. Recent work continues to refer back to her pioneering reports and these remain a major contribution to this area. Kübler-Ross is a Swiss psychiatrist who published her very influential book, *On Death and Dying* in 1969. In this book Kübler-Ross describes the experience of someone facing their own death in terms of five stages. Kübler-Ross based her study on extensive contact with dying patients and she found that as patients experienced these different stages she was able to engage them in different types of communication, a point that we will examine more closely in the next section. The five stages she described are as follows:

First Stage: Denial. Kübler-Ross observed that when her patients first became aware that their condition was fatal the initial reaction was one of disbelief. They simply could not believe it. She suggests that this is an important and helpful initial response as it allows time for the reality to sink in gradually. Someone facing their own death is faced with the loss of everything. Even if a person is convinced of an afterlife they still face separation from everything they have loved and valued in this world. The implications of this are best acknowledged gradually. Although people demonstrate denial in many different ways, the basic response is: 'This isn't happening to me, there must be some mistake'. To some extent this response persists through all five stages. With most people a glimmer of hope persists that the disease will be reversed either by a cure or by remission. But this persistent glimmer of hope is not denial. Denial involves turning away from the truth. Patients may refuse to talk about their condition, withdraw, and insist that they will soon be well. This can continue for weeks, or even months. In her work Kübler-Ross did not attempt to force patients to face the reality of their condition. Her approach was to signal her willingness to be open and responsive to those patients, and then allow them to open up in their own time. As Kübler-Ross notes, very few patients will remain in this stage of denial right up to their death.

Second Stage: Anger. After an initial period of denial, Kübler-Ross describes a stage in which the patient becomes very angry and resentful. The patient realises that it is not a mistake, that they really are dying. Often there is then a sense of injustice and anger as the patient asks: 'Why me?' Of course people will vary in the degree to which they feel such resentment. In general younger people appear to react particularly strongly, as they feel cheated of their life. The targets of hostility can be professionals who the patient feels are not doing their job properly; relatives who may be accused of being uncaring or insensitive; God for allowing the trauma to occur; and perhaps anyone who isn't in the same position as the patient. Clearly this can be a very difficult time for communication between patient and relatives or friends, who may bear the brunt of the patient's anger.

Third Stage: Bargaining. Kübler-Ross describes the third stage as one in which the patient tries to 'buy' extra time by striking up some kind of bargain. It's as if the second stage of anger involved some attempt through protest to change what is happening, as if this anger was a demand for justice and fairness. When this strategy fails it's as if some people try to trade improvement in their circumstances for good behaviour: 'If God (or the doctors) will just give me another six months so I can see my child start school, I will promise to donate money to the poor, or donate my body to medical science'. When a patient is attempting to postpone the inevitable in this way it can be difficult to communicate because the state of mind identified by Kübler-Ross as that of 'Bargaining' involves the postponement of considering the implications of death. Although the patient may be calm, they will rarely be amenable to taking about their feelings, or the practical affairs that relatives may want to discuss. 'Bargaining' retains strong features of denial, and as such is a barrier to open communication. Once again Kübler-Ross suggests allowing the patient to indulge this strategy and remaining available to respond when the patient realises that 'Bargaining' is not going to work.

Fourth Stage: Depression. When someone is dying they are faced with the loss of everything. It is not surprising that dying people commonly react with denial or anger, or attempt to 'bargain' their way out of their situation. When these responses fail to change their condition, the dying person may finally become depressed, withdrawn and be unwilling to see anyone. There may be overt expressions of grief, such as intense and prolonged sobbing. Relatives and friends will naturally find it very distressing to be with a patient when they are experiencing such sorrow. But it is unwise to try to stop the patient feeling sad, or to turn away from them. As Kübler-Ross emphasises, if a patient can experience and express their sadness it will help them to move beyond the experience of depression to that of acceptance.

Fifth Stage: Acceptance. Kübler-Ross described the stage of acceptance as coming when the difficult experiences and feelings associated with earlier stages have been worked through. Acceptance is not itself a feeling, it is more a state of mind in which the person has ceased to struggle against death. This stage is characterised by an acceptance of the inevitability of death, and a willingness for it to be so. The illusions of 'Denial' and 'Bargaining', the turmoil of 'Anger' and the sorrow of 'Depression' have passed, and there remains a recognition and calm acceptance of the reality of approaching death. In Kübler-Ross's description this stage is often accompanied by a tendency to refrain from speech, where non-verbal communication – in the form of being a supportive presence to the person – acquires great significance. It is as if words become too clumsy. In contrast to the clumsiness of speech, holding the patient's hand could 'say' more than hours of talk. By this stage many of Kübler-Ross's patients had a sense of completion, that what needed to be done had been done, what needed to be said had been said. Nothing remained but to accept the inevitable.

The description of these five stages provided by Kübler-Ross has been a major contribution to a growing awareness of the range of responses that someone facing their own death is likely to experience. It is interesting to compare these five stages with the Four Phases of Mourning described by Bowlby, which we considered in chapter 1. It will be noted that they are very similar. This similarity is not surprising when you consider someone facing their own death and someone mourning the death of a loved one are both struggling to come to terms with very significant experiences of loss. Losses on this scale require similar painful adjustments, in which a person's identity and view of the world will undergo dramatic change. Just as we can note the similarities between Kübler-Ross's 'Stages' of dying, and Bowlby's 'Phases' of mourning, it is important to note that the reservations mentioned in connection with the latter apply just as much to the former. People respond differently. It would be a serious mistake to imagine that everyone facing their own death goes through these five stages in orderly succession. People react in their individual and unique ways. Some will show features of all these stages, others will not. Some may move in and out of the various stages in rapid succession, others will seem to be stuck in one stage – for example, showing a predominance of anger. Some may experience the sequence as described by Kübler-Ross but many experience only some of the stages; perhaps in a different order or perhaps aspects of two or more apparently at the same time. The idea of 'Stages' of dying becomes very misleading and unhelpful if we assume there is a set sequence that it would be 'abnormal' not to follow as described. However, Kübler-Ross's work can be of great value if we bear in mind the following essential points. Firstly, a person's response will change and these changes represent attempts to come to terms with the fact that they are dying. Secondly, while these changing moods can certainly make communication difficult, if we can understand the struggle that the dying person is experiencing and not take affront at their manner but remain available and ready to respond, we can provide them with valuable support in their struggle.

Communicating with someone who is dying

Kübler-Ross's work is a useful background for the delicate topic of communicating with someone who is dying. Her work helps us to understand the struggle the dying person may be experiencing. Further, an awareness of the general features of the five stages, or responses, can provide helpful guidelines to the type of communication that is and is not possible with the dying person. What complicates this issue, of course, is the fact that those close to the dying person will also be experiencing various aspects of anticipatory grief and mourning which may be similar to some of the experiences of the person who is dying. Patterns of communication vary widely. Some relationships involve open expression of thoughts and feelings, both critical and affectionate, while other relationships tend to avoid such exchanges. It would not be helpful to try to give rules about what and how to communicate. But there are some general principles that may help facilitate communication with someone who is dying.

Communicating with someone who is dying can often be very difficult. No-one would pretend that witnessing the struggle and suffering of a loved person, and simultaneously struggling with one's own impending loss, can be anything but excruciatingly painful. And yet the distress can be lessened, and strength found, in moments when genuine, honest communication is possible. Such moments of contact and human closeness can be among life's most precious experiences.

When considering the responses described by Kübler-Ross questions about what should be communicated naturally arise. For example, if a patient appears to be denying the reality of their situation, or attempting to 'bargain' their way out of it, should they be challenged? As we have noted, Kübler-Ross does not advocate confronting patients who display these responses. Her approach is not to collude with their responses but to convey her willingness to talk, inviting the patient to express what they are feeling, and allow them to open up in their own time. People try to avoid facing reality because it is painful; it will not help if someone, in misguided enthusiasm for 'the truth', attempts to force their awareness before they are ready.

An anxiety that is often expressed by relatives and friends of someone who is dying is that talking to the person about their condition may make them more distressed. The worry is that focusing on feelings, and inviting the patient to express themselves, could make the patient worse. This is, of course, an understandable concern, but research has repeatedly shown that most dying people actually experience less fear, anxiety and depression if they are able to communicate their concerns to others and be genuinely heard. By contrast it appears that silence and avoidance on the part of others creates isolation and distress in the patient.

Kübler-Ross's descriptions of patients' anger and depression (which she describes in her second and fourth stages of dying) note how difficult communication can be at these times. It can be very painful for relatives and friends, who are attempting to cope with their own feelings about their anticipated loss, to be on the receiving end of a patient's anger, or find them unresponsive to their attempts to offer support and help. Here again it is important to try to understand what the dying person is experiencing. Anger and unresponsiveness may appear to be directed at an individual for some failing or error. However, these feelings need to be put into the context of a person's struggle to come to terms with death. A dying person experiencing these feelings is unlikely to be helped by counter-attacks, or accusations, or admonitions to 'snap out of it'. It is also usually unhelpful to say: 'I know how you feel'. It is usually much more helpful to be present, trying to accept the patient's feelings and expressions of distress as being about their condition rather than being personal attacks, showing support and warmth, perhaps by holding their hand, and acknowledging their feelings with simple statements which do not blame or contradict. These are more likely to be experienced by the dying person as supportive and caring responses that help them feel they are not being left to struggle with their pain alone.

There are certainly difficulties in communicating with a patient who is responding with marked denial, anger, bargaining or depression, but these responses need not be regarded as complete blocks to communication. The point is to communicate with the dying person as openly as possible, while recognising that the level of communication will probably vary considerably as the dying person struggles with the reality of the situation. Many of those who have spent time with a loved one during a terminal illness describe the sharing of memories as particularly poignant. This may provoke tears, but is often experienced as contributing to a sense of completion, of consummation, and a source of fond memory after the death has occurred. It is important to remember that communication does not just mean talking. The dying person may not want to talk, or there may seem to be little to say. But physical expressions of support and affection – such as holding hands, a kiss, squeezing someone's arm, a smile – have meaning and can be powerful forms of communication.

Has the dying person made a will?

Although it can seem inappropriate, morbid, or perhaps even 'mercenary' (that is, motivated by a desire for personal profit) to broach this subject with someone who is dying, it is important to remember that only about one in three adults in Britain has a will, and that if someone dies without making a valid will the state will dispose of the deceased's possessions in a way dictated by law, according to strict rules. In the absence of a valid will specifying what is to happen to the deceased's possessions, property and savings, the wishes of the survivors, or even the wishes the deceased may have expressed verbally, have no legal force whatsoever. The law will not take into account reports of what the deceased may have said they would like to happen to their savings or possessions, or what may have been promised to certain people. Without a valid will the state will follow clear rules for disposing of the deceased's 'estate' (which simply means everything a person owns: savings, investments, property and possessions, whether these be meagre or substantial).

Hence the only way to ensure that possessions are disposed of according to the wishes of the deceased is to make sure there is a valid will. Asking if the dying person would like help in this matter so that their wishes are carried out is a service to them.

Before describing how to make a valid will let us consider for a moment what happens when someone dies without one. First, all debts and liabilities will be settled from the estate. What is left will be disposed of according to rules laid down in law (the Administration of Estates Act, for residents of England and Wales). If the deceased was married and the value of the estate – that is, the total value of everything after payment of debts and liabilities – is less than £75,000, the entire estate will go automatically to the surviving spouse. No-one else, including children and parents, will have a legal claim on the estate. If a couple have joint home ownership the surviving spouse's share will not be included in the estate; this goes automatically to the surviving spouse. Note that these rules apply only to a legal spouse. This rule does not apply to couples who may be living together but are not married. Hence if someone is living separately from their legal spouse, with another partner, the law still legislates that the estate must go to the legal spouse.

If the total value of the estate is over £75,000 it will be divided according to strict rules. Assuming the deceased was married with children, the surviving spouse will get the first £75,000 plus household and personal possessions. The rest of the estate will be divided into two equal parts. One half will be divided equally among the children (who will be eligible to receive this when they are eighteen years old). The second half will be put into a trust for the surviving spouse, from which the interest can be drawn but not the basic capital investment. This capital is preserved for the children who will receive equal amounts after the surviving spouse also dies. If the deceased was married but had no children, their spouse will receive the first £125,000, plus personal possessions, and half of whatever else remains. The other half will go to relatives in the following order, depending on who survives the deceased: parents, brothers and sisters, nieces and nephews.

If the deceased has no legal spouse their estate will be divided equally among the surviving children. If the deceased has no children the estate will go to relatives in the following order, depending on who survives the deceased: parents, brothers and sisters, grandparents, uncles and aunts, nephews and nieces, cousins. If there are no living relations all of the estate will go to the Crown. Once again it is important to note that the law specifies *legal* spouse. Even if the deceased has lived with a partner for many years they will not receive anything.

The rules of the Administration of Estates Act are rigidly applied and it is easy to see how situations can arise in which survivors feel either unjustly treated or that the deceased's wishes have not been implemented. You may look over these rules and feel that they would, in fact, implement the wishes of a person who is dying, that their estate would go to those they would want to receive it. But making such an assumption is a risk. Circumstances change and difficulties do arise. The only way to avoid such problems is to make sure a valid will is drawn up which clearly specifies how the estate should be disposed of. This one act of making a valid will can save the deceased's relatives a great deal of avoidable distress.

Drawing up a will is an opportunity to make wishes explicit, and is essential if it is desired that the estate, or parts of the estate, should go to someone such as a partner to whom the deceased was not married, or to an institution, such as a charity. The will also provides an opportunity to specify what type of funeral is desired, and indicate any wishes regarding donations of the body or body parts to medicine. Guardians can also be appointed for children under eighteen, and the person can be specified who is to act as an 'executor' or 'personal administrator', whose job is to oversee the implementation of the will. Any personal preferences about these issues must be made explicit in a valid will otherwise these wishes will not be implemented.

Essentially there are four steps to drawing up a will:

1 Make an estimate of the value of the estate. List all assets: house, car, possessions, savings, investments, insurance, pensions, benefits, etc. Then list all liabilities: mortgage, loans, debts, etc. Subtracting the liabilities from the assets gives the net value of the estate.

2 Decide how the estate should be divided, who should receive what. It must be decided who is to receive money, property, or possessions from the estate. The estate can be divided however is desired; institutions like charities, as well as individuals, can be included. Money or property can be left 'in trust' for children or grandchildren, with a stipulation of the age at which they should receive what has been left. Preferences for funeral arrangements, and organ or body donations, can also be included in the will.

3 Decide who will be the 'executor' of the estate. The 'executor' is the person who is to deal with the details of implementing the will: he or she is actually named in the will. (In fact more than one executor can be named.) The executor can be a spouse, or a member of the family or a friend. As the executor will be carrying out the instructions contained in the will it is helpful to discuss the details with them. The executor must apply for a Grant of Probate, which simply provides the formal acknowledgement of the executor's position as the personal representative of the deceased, and also formally recognises the will in the local Probate Registry. The executor must ensure that the deceased's debts are paid and their assets disposed of according to the instructions in the will. The costs incurred by the executors in the administration of the will, including funeral arrangements, telephone calls and travelling expenses, are all considered liabilities of the deceased and hence can be subtracted from their estate (as such they are also tax deductible). As the administration of an estate can be complex it is advisable to discuss the details with the named executor to make sure they are willing to accept the responsibility.

4 Choose a solicitor. A will can be made without a solicitor by purchasing the appropriate form from a stationer. However, there are numerous difficulties that can arise: for example, being unfamiliar with the details of the rights of dependents to challenge the will if they deem it unfair; the effects of divorce or remarriage on the will; failing to follow the correct procedure for altering the will; failing to ensure the will is correctly signed and witnessed; failing to consider contingencies such as the deaths of beneficiaries before implementation of the will; and failing to give instructions covering all of one's assets. If the will is likely to be complex it is advisable to consult a solicitor: he or she will be able to offer reliable advice on these and other details to make sure the will expresses instructions and wishes accurately and comprehensively, and meets all the requirements for it to be legally valid. Solicitors' fees vary, and it is a good idea to obtain estimates from a number before making a choice. Most solicitors charge about £60 for drawing up a will. The charity Age Concern charges about £40 for drawing up a will, which they can do from a questionnaire. The Will Registry charges about £30 for drafting a will, also based on a questionnaire. (Both of these addresses are given in Appendix 1 at the end of this book.)

To return to the point made at the beginning of this section, many people may feel reluctant to discuss matters such as making a will with someone who is dying, and there is certainly need for tact in choosing the right time to do so. But it is worth bearing in mind that the only way to ensure that the wishes of the person regarding their estate are carried out after their death is to leave these wishes clearly recorded in a valid will. It is also worth noting the comments in the publication *Wills and Probate* edited by the Consumers' Association: 'The one thing worse than not making a will at all is making a mess of making a will'.

Dying at home

At present in Britain about 70% of patients die in hospital, about 10% in other institutional settings such as hospices, and about 20% die at home. The trend towards more people dying in hospital is clear: in 1960 less than 50% of deaths occurred in hospital. However, when asked to express a preference most people, about 80%, say they would prefer to die at home in familiar surroundings with family and close friends present.

In Britain the main obstacle to dying at home concerns the practicalities of care, which can be considerable. Legally a person can discharge themselves from hospital, even if this is against medical advice. Where a patient is not able to decide or communicate their wishes the dying person's family can decide to take them home. It may be possible to check the patient's wishes by asking them to indicate a 'Yes' (or a 'No') by squeezing a hand, raising a finger, or blinking. If this step is being considered it is important to anticipate what will be involved. Are there enough carers to make sure the patient's needs are attended to? The amount of work involved in looking after a terminally ill patient at home should not be underestimated. It is important to be clear about special food and drink requirements, medication (especially pain control), cleanliness and hygiene, the prevention of bedsores, toileting and other factors bearing on the physical comfort of the patient. Medical staff will be able to provide details of the level of care that will be needed. It must be remembered that the priority is no longer 'finding a cure', but providing the conditions that allow the patient to die with as much comfort and dignity as possible.

It should be possible to arrange nursing care and support, depending on what is available locally. In addition to NHS provisions for nursing care at home, Social Services or local voluntary agencies may be able to provide various forms of practical assistance such as home help, laundry services, and delivery of meals to the home. Macmillan Nurses receive specialised training in the care of cancer patients and their home visits can be an invaluable means of support. Similarly Marie Curie Nurses may be available locally, and can arrange to stay with patients all night if this is needed. Financial assistance is also available for help with prescriptions (form FP91 from post offices or GP's surgery) and attendance allowances (these are not means tested and application forms are available from local Social Security Offices). Much depends on what is available locally, and it is important to try to get as clear a picture as possible of what help will be required and then to make specific requests through a GP and the various agencies that operate locally. Addresses and telephone numbers of agencies mentioned here are provided in Appendix 1.

The practical demands on carers, even with nursing and support from social services, are often considerable, but there are of course even greater emotional demands. Once again these should not be underestimated, and it is important that carers take advantage of whatever support is available locally.

Rosalind was thirty-two when her husband, Joshua, was told he had liver cancer. They had three young children, and were in the middle of renovating a large country house. Rosalind had always been extremely hard-working and was devoted to her family. She had experienced many difficulties and disadvantages in her life, having been severely abused by both of her parents, thus spending much of her childhood in children's homes. Rosalind married Joshua when she was twenty-three and Joshua was thirty-four. Joshua's brother had died at home after a long illness and Joshua was convinced that it had been an important and vital experience for his brother and all the family. In some way his brother's presence, and the expectancy of his death, had moved the family towards greater intimacy and honesty than had been possible for years. Both Rosalind and Joshua were determined that Joshua should die at home. But Rosalind was also determined that she should take charge, as far as possible, of all Joshua's needs – physical, emotional and spiritual. She was very reluctant to accept the various forms of support and practical assistance suggested by her GP. Although regular visits from a district nurse were arranged, and medication for the control of Joshua's pain and the reduction of nausea and constipation was carefully monitored, Rosalind took responsibility for everything else. Needless to say, along with caring for three young children and the difficulty of arranging for urgent work that needed to be done on the house, Rosalind found herself struggling to provide the care that she wanted for her husband. During the three months Joshua was cared for at home both Rosalind and her husband were able to prepare themselves and share their mutual grief and mourning. Rosalind felt it was good for the family to be together during this period and did not regret the decision to care for Joshua at home.

However, the weight of the responsibilities Rosalind took upon herself were clearly evident. Rosalind was very distressed by feelings of being overwhelmed by the volume of work and things that needed her attention. She found herself experiencing moods of resentment and anger that she should be in such a position. Despite her attempts to fight against her feelings she found herself feeling anger towards Joshua, almost as if emotionally she was experiencing his illness as a deliberate abandonment of her. At times she found herself wishing it was over, in effect willing that his death would come soon. These feelings, in appearance so contradictory to her deep love for her husband, were a source of guilt and shame and caused a great deal of distress. Such feelings are, of course, understandable in these circumstances and it is a great pity that Rosalind did not allow herself to take advantage of the various avenues of support available in her area. Although such help, both practical and emotional, can never make the experience of caring for a terminally ill person easy, it can help to make such experiences very much more manageable.

If it is not possible to care adequately for the dying person in their own home or the home of a friend or relative, and a place is not available in a hospice, arrangements will need to be made with some other institution. Hospitals, day care centres, or residential homes are probably the most familiar options. But there may well be several possibilities, and it is worth discussing the options with a GP.

A 'Good Death'

In 1491 a book was published in London which we now call *The Book on the Art of Dying* (at the time it was called *Art and Craft to know ye Well to Dye*). The book remained in print, going through numerous editions, for several hundred years. The belief that there could be an 'art' to dying, that death could be faced with varying degrees of skill, was virtually universal throughout Europe until the nineteenth century. Under the influence of Christianity the idea of a 'Good Death' involved beliefs about dying in a condition acceptable to God, in a 'state of grace', which would ensure passage from this world of pain and suffering into another world of bliss. However, with the growing influence of medical science and the decline of Christianity, the idea of a 'Good Death' underwent changes. For most people living in Britain the notion of a 'Good Death' has been stripped of both its religious associations, and the idea that there could be a skill or art to dying. Death without pain, in peace, without regrets, having made peace with others and said farewells, is a description of what many would consider to be a 'Good Death'. However, having given many lectures and workshops on this subject I am always intrigued to discover how varied people's notions are of what a 'Good Death' would be. Some regard a sudden, painless death to be far more acceptable than actually knowing that you are about to die. Others feel an essential aspect of a 'Good Death' is to have control over the process; that is, being able to decide where, when and how to die. Some regard being conscious and able to communicate in their last hours as vital, others are much more concerned with being free of pain. It is interesting to note that people's ideas of what constitutes a 'Good Death' vary depending on whether they are asked what would be a 'Good Death' for themselves, or what they would regard as a 'Good Death' for someone they love. Differences are also apparent between various professions that have contact with the dying. Doctors, nurses, clergy, undertakers and psychotherapists often have differing views of what constitutes a 'Good Death'. Clearly, in view of such variations in notions of what it means to have a 'Good Death', it would be unwise to assume others will have a similar view to ourselves, and even more unhelpful to try to impose our view on someone else.

In Britain the hospice movement has done a great deal to increase awareness of the quality of life for those who are dying. Hospice care (both residential and home help) combines careful attention to the physical aspects of terminal illness (notably pain control and physical comfort) with an equal focus on its psychological aspects. Staff involved in hospice care are trained to be sensitive to the difficult feelings that people often experience as they approach the end of their life. But they are also aware of the importance of family interactions at this time. The kind of issues raised in this chapter will be familiar to hospice staff. With their training and experience they can often provide conditions where families are helped to make use of the time they have left together. Part of the aim of hospice care is to help people to 'die their own death'. That is, there is no single way to die that everyone is expected to conform to. For many, a 'Good Death' would involve dying with as much comfort and dignity and personal choice as possible. Some people may want an explicit, perhaps formal religious focus, others do not. Such differences are recognised and valued in the hospice movement. Information about local hospice services can be obtained from the hospice information service, whose address and telephone number can be found in Appendix 1.

Many publications that have come out of the 'death awareness' movement have focused on accounts, both historical and contemporary which offer models of a 'Good Death', often stressing acceptance, openness, lack of resistance and regrets, consciousness, and a willingness to enter the unknown. Such accounts can, of course, be intimidating quite as often as they may be inspiring. It would be an unfortunate error of judgement if such accounts led one to try to impose a way of dying on another person. To repeat the above point: each person must die their own death. Robert Buckman in his book, *I Don't Know What To Say*, has rightly observed: 'It should be your objective to help your friend let go of life *in his own way*. It may not be your way, and it may not be the way you read about in a book or magazine, but it is his way'. It would not be helpful to try to impose a way of dying on another person; no-one has the responsibility or the right to do that.

Summary

In this chapter we have considered anticipatory grief and mourning as being a time of opportunity as well as sadness. Preparing for loss naturally involves grief and sorrow, but there is also hope and the possibility of consummation. Much of the material in this chapter has been about communication between those to be bereaved and the dying person. Despite the difficulties that may arise the rewards of such communication, for both the dying person and those who will mourn their death, can be considerable.

6 What to do when someone dies

In this chapter we will consider what needs to be done when someone dies. If you have not been through this experience yourself you may be very surprised at the number of things that have to be done after a death occurs. There are people to be notified, paperwork to be completed, decisions to be made regarding funeral arrangements and the disposal of possessions, and many other details that need to be attended to. Someone who has just suffered the loss of a loved person has to face the stress of dealing with all these things, which will require a considerable amount of time and energy to sort out. The bereaved person may be in a state of shock or depression and find the strain of dealing with these things overwhelming. The bereaved person will usually find assistance with all of these details very helpful. For example, help completing paperwork, notifying people and getting to various agencies, such as the Registry office, can lighten the burden considerably. Relatives or friends can offer valuable help, but it should also be borne in mind that having to focus on the practical decisions and arrangements that need to be made can actually help the bereaved person adjust to their loss. A balance between personal involvement along with support and assistance with practicalities is likely to be most helpful for the bereaved person. This chapter provides guidelines covering the most important things which need to be done after someone dies. More detailed information is available in the booklet *What to do after a death* issued by the Department of Social Security (**Leaflet D49**). This publication is available free of charge from the Department of Social Security. (The procedures are slightly different in Scotland and a booklet is available that covers this.)

Saying goodbye

In recent years an increasing amount of attention has been paid to the importance of saying goodbye to the person who has died. Most researchers and counsellors in this field suggest that, particularly when the loss has not been anticipated, this is most effectively done when actually seeing the body. Many bereaved people report spending some time alone with the body, perhaps on more than one occasion, to be very helpful. It is an opportunity to express thoughts and feelings to the deceased, and, as some therapists term it, 'deal with unfinished business'. The body can be seen anytime between the death and the funeral. Whether in a hospital mortuary, or an undertaker's chapel, or in the deceased's own home, it is suggested that mourners are at least given the opportunity to see the body even though they may decide not to. Although there is more disagreement about whether children should see the body, once again most workers in this field suggest that many children do find it helpful, and therefore should at least be given the opportunity. But of course no child (and for that matter no adult) should ever be compelled to see the remains of someone who has died. If a child does choose to see the body it is advisable that they are accompanied by at least one adult. Deciding whether nor not to see the body, whether it will in fact be helpful in coming to terms with the loss, is a more complex issue if the body has been disfigured in some way. Certainly there are situations where seeing the remains of a loved one will actually add to the trauma of the loss, rather than be helpful. It is advisable in these circumstances to talk to someone with experience in these matters, perhaps a doctor or hospital chaplain, before seeing the remains.

Some people find the funeral offers an opportunity to say farewell to the deceased before the body is taken, put into the ground, or cremated. There is often a strong sense of departure, of separation from the deceased. As such, the funeral is for many people the best point to say goodbye. This of course needs to be done in their own way: it is not the method that is crucial. Saying goodbye to the deceased, in whatever way it is done, can reinforce the reality of the loss and facilitate grief. That is, saying goodbye to the deceased can form an important part of adapting to the loss.

Who should be informed?

About 80% of deaths in Britain occur in a hospital or other institution. When death occurs in hospital the next of kin will usually be informed by the senior nurse. If the death has occurred as a result of an accident the police will be informed, and the body will have to be identified, usually by a relative.

If the death occurs at home the GP should be informed, as well as close relatives.

After these initial contacts there are a number of other people who will need to be informed of the death. Here is a check list:

- Executor(s) of the will.
- The deceased's employer.
- Any professional bodies of which the deceased was a member.
- Trade union.
- The Unemployment Benefit Office, if the deceased was unemployed.
- Any school, college or university that the deceased was attending.
- The local authority, if the deceased was in receipt of a grant.
- The deceased's landlord.
- The local council Housing Department, if the deceased was a council tenant.
- The local Housing Benefit/Council Tax Benefit Department.
- The Social Security Office, if the deceased received payments such as Retirement Pension or Attendance Allowance.
- The Social Services Department.
- The local offices of British Gas.
- The local electricity office.
- The telephone company.
- Car insurance company (someone insured to drive the car under the deceased's name will no longer be legally insured).
- House and house contents insurance company.
- Life insurance company.
- Pensions group.
- The relevant Tax Office. (If the address cannot be found in the deceased's papers it will be in the telephone book under *Inland Revenue*. If more information on tax is needed the Inland Revenue can provide a leaflet: **IR45** *What happens when someone dies*.)
- The local Social Services Department, if the deceased was

getting meals-on-wheels, home help or day centre care, or had an appliance or piece of equipment issued by the Department.
- The Post Office, if the deceased's mail is to be redirected.
- Any hospital or specialist clinic the deceased was attending, including dentists and opticians.
- The deceased's bank.
- The deceased's building society.
- The deceased's mortgage company.
- The deceased's credit card company.
- Anyone to whom debts are outstanding.

The following documents should be returned to the appropriate authority with a letter explaining that the person concerned has died, giving the date of death:

- Order books, payable orders, or girocheques should be sent to the Social Security Office (or the DSS office which issued payment).
- The deceased's passport should be sent to the Passport Office (the address of the Passport Office is available from any post office).
- The deceased's driving licence should be sent to DVLC, Swansea SA6 7GL.
- Car registration documents should be sent for change in ownership to be recorded.
- National Insurance papers should be sent to the relevant office.
- Any membership cards of clubs and associations should be returned with a request for refund (if applicable).
- Any season tickets should be returned with a request for refund (if applicable).
- Library books and tickets should be returned.

The personal representative

If there is a will it should name an **executor** or **executors**. As noted in the last chapter this is the person or persons the deceased nominated to ensure that the instructions in the will are carried out. The executor must apply to a Probate Registry Office for a **Grant of Probate**. This is a formal recognition of the will in the local Probate Registry, and authorises the executor to 'administer the estate'. The 'estate' refers to the deceased's money, property and possessions. In addition to carrying out whatever instructions are contained in the will, the executor is responsible for dealing with the financial matters arising from the death. This includes paying off debts, taxes, and expenses such as the funeral. Where a will has not been left someone must apply for **Letters of Administration**, which authorise the person concerned to act as **administrator** of the estate. The administrator is then responsible for financial matters. It should be noted that the various financial commitments, such as the deceased's debts and costs for the funeral, are to be paid for from the deceased's estate. The executor (named in a will), or the administrator (appointed through application in the absence of a will), is also known as the **personal representative**.

Administering an estate can be complex and in some cases it may be advisable to employ a solicitor. However, solicitors can be very expensive so it is worth checking a number of solicitors before deciding. If the personal representative (executor or administrator) decides not to employ a solicitor, **Form PA2,** obtainable from the Probate Registry Office, will explain how to proceed with administering the estate. Banks and building societies will normally release money from the deceased's account, but will need to be consulted for details on how this is to be done. When all the debts, taxes, and expenses (including the funeral) have been paid, the personal representative can distribute what is left of the estate. In the case of the executor this will be done according to the instructions in the will; and in the case of the administrator, according to strict rules (some of which were outlined in chapter 5).

The Medical Certificate and Formal Notice

All deaths require a **Medical Certificate** stating the causes of death. The Medical Certificate must be completed by a doctor who knows the cause of death. This will usually be the family GP, or the doctor who attended the deceased in hospital. When the cause of death is known the Medical Certificate will be completed by a doctor and will be given to the next of kin in a sealed envelope, addressed to the Registrar. Where a baby is stillborn the doctor or midwife issues a Medical Certificate of stillbirth.

Along with the Medical Certificate the next of kin will be

given a **Formal Notice** (or 'notice to informant'; the informant is the person who goes to register the death). The Formal Notice simply confirms that the doctor has completed the Medical Certificate stating the cause of death, and explains how to register the death. There is no charge for these two forms.

If the body is to be cremated, a second doctor must complete a second form confirming the cause of death. This is necessary because once a body has been cremated it cannot, of course, be re-examined if a question about the cause of death arises later. The requirement that two doctors complete separate forms is to ensure that the cause of death is known for certain before the cremation can go ahead.

If the cause of death is unclear there will be a delay in issuing the Medical Certificate until the cause can be ascertained. In these circumstances a coroner is notified (see below under *The coroner*). In some circumstances the hospital doctors may want to know more about the cause of death and the next of kin will be asked for permission to carry out a post-mortem examination of the body. This will involve cutting the body to obtain a clearer picture of the cause of death. Relatives can refuse to give permission for this.

Registering the death

Deaths have to be registered by the Registrar of Births and Deaths within five days. To register a death you must take the envelope containing the Medical Certificate stating the cause of death (which will be in an envelope addressed to the Registrar) to the **Registry Office** of the area in which the death occurred. The address of the Registry Office can be found in the telephone book under *Registration of Births, Deaths and Marriages*. The address should also be available from the doctor, local council, a post office or police station. The Formal Notice, which is given along with the Medical Certificate, explains how to register the death. It is best to find out when the Registrar will be available, and to check who is eligible to sign the register of death. As no appointments are made there may be a long wait at the office. The Registrar will want the Medical Certificate stating the cause of death and the following documents belonging to the deceased:

- Medical Card.
- Birth Certificate.
- Marriage Certificate.
- War Pension book.
- A 'Pink Form' if the coroner has been involved and ordered a post-mortem examination (see section below, *The coroner*).

The Registrar will want to know the following details:

- The date and place of death.
- The deceased's last (usual) address.
- The deceased's first names and surname (and maiden name where applicable).
- The deceased's date and place of birth (town and county, and, if born abroad, country).
- The deceased's occupation (and the name and occupation of her husband if applicable).
- Whether the deceased received a state pension or other allowances.
- If the deceased was married (and the date of birth of the surviving widow or widower).

The Registrar will issue two certificates. First, a **Certificate for Burial or Cremation**. The certificate must be given to the funeral director as a body cannot be buried or cremated without it. The second is a **Certificate of Registration of Death**. This is for use in notifying the Department of Society Security if this is necessary. Instructions are provided on the back of the certificate. If any of the instructions apply the certificate should be completed and sent to the Social Security Office. There is no charge for these two certificates.

The Registrar can also provide copies of the **Death Certificate**. The Death Certificate is a certified copy of the entry in the death register. Copies may be needed for the will, or to make pension or insurance claims, or claim savings certificates and premium bonds. There is a fee for copies of the Death Certificate and it is best to obtain as many copies as are needed, as the price of copies increases if you apply for one later.

The coroner

The coroner is a doctor or lawyer whose job is to investigate deaths which occur in the following circumstances:

- The cause of death is unknown or uncertain.
- The death was a result of violence.
- The death resulted from an accident.
- The death was caused by an industrial disease.
- The death occurred whilst the deceased was in prison or police custody.
- The death occurred during or within twenty four hours of an operation.
- The death was the result of military action.
- The death was the result of suicide.
- The death was due to abortion.
- The circumstances surrounding the death were suspicious.

If a doctor decides, for whatever reason, to report the death to the coroner, he or she will write on the Formal Notice that the death has been referred to the coroner. In these circumstances the Medical Certificate cannot be issued until the coroner reaches a decision. In most cases notifying the coroner is merely routine and the coroner will usually not recommend further investigations. In such cases the coroner simply notifies the Registrar that the death can be registered by the informant (that is, the person who goes to register the death). In this case the coroner sends the Registrar form 100, also called the **Pink Form**, or the **Notification by the Coroner**. But where the coroner does recommend further investigation (usually this happens when the cause of death is unknown) registering the death will be delayed. The coroner can provide an interim death certificate that will allow the process of disposing of the deceased's estate to begin. Enquiries can be made to the coroner's office; the address should be available from the police station, or if the death occurred in hospital from the hospital office dealing with deaths.

When a coroner orders a post-mortem examination of the body the purpose is to establish the cause of death. This can be done without the permission of relatives, and the coroner will not generally inform the family of the results of the post-mortem. Once the results are known – that is, the cause of death has been established – the coroner will authorise the Registrar to issue the death certificate. Although the Registrar may contact the next of kin when such authorisation is received it is often left up to the relatives to contact either the coroner, to see if the authorisation has been sent, or the Registrar to see if it has been received. Once the authorisation from the coroner is received the Registrar can issue the death certificate to the informant, in the same way as noted above. If the body is to be cremated the coroner will also provide the Certificate for Cremation.

Inquests

Sometimes the coroner will hold an inquest into the cause and circumstances of death. The coroner will hold an inquest if the death has occurred in any of the following circumstances:

- The death resulted from violence or an accident.
- The death occurred in prison.
- The death was caused by an industrial disease.
- The cause of death remains uncertain even after post-mortem examination.

If an inquest is held the coroner will inform the deceased's next of kin, or personal representative.

Although the way in which the inquest is conducted varies, it is essentially a court of law and is open to the public. It may include a jury. Relatives can attend and question witnesses about the circumstances and causes of death. Evidence, including the testimony of witnesses, will be presented to the coroner, and to the jury if there is one. The aim of this procedure is solely to establish the cause and circumstances of the death; it is not to establish whether a crime has been committed. In cases involving claims for compensation (including road or industrial accidents) relatives are advised to arrange for a lawyer to be present to represent them (although it should be noted that legal aid is not available for this). After the inquest the coroner will send a **Certificate After Inquest** which states the cause of death to the Registrar. Once the Registrar receives this certificate the death can be registered. The coroner will return an open verdict if the evidence presented is insufficient to establish the cause or the circumstances of the death. Inquiries can take some time to complete, in which case it is usually possible to obtain from the coroner a letter confirming the death which can be sent to Social Security and National Insurance offices, and either an **Order for Burial** or a **Certificate for Cremation**, which can be given to the funeral director so that the funeral is not delayed further.

Arranging the funeral

Before making any funeral arrangements the following questions should be considered:

1 Did the deceased leave any instructions about funeral arrangements? The deceased's will and papers should be checked to see if he or she had arranged space for burial in a churchyard or cemetery. If there are no instructions, or if for some reason the deceased's instructions are to be disregarded (it should be noted that the deceased's instructions regarding funeral arrangements have no legal force), it is the next of kin, or the personal representative, who must decide on funeral arrangements.

2 How will the funeral arrangements be paid for? Funerals typically cost between £500 and £1,500. The costs cover details such as the transportation and preparation of the body, the coffin, coffin bearers, the fee for whoever conducts the service (usually a member of the clergy) and the cost of the actual burial or cremation. The will and the deceased's papers should be checked to see if any arrangements had been made prior to the death. There may be insurance policies or pension schemes which cover the funeral costs. If no provisions have been made, the cost of the funeral is deductible from the deceased's estate. If the deceased did not leave sufficient funds, whoever arranges the funeral will be eligible to pay the cost. It is possible to get help with paying for a funeral through the Social Security system; advice on making a claim will be available from any Social Security Office or Citizens' Advice Bureau. Where the deceased's relations cannot be traced, or cannot pay, the local council or the health authority may arrange for a basic funeral.

The costs can be claimed for the deceased's estate where there are funds sufficient to cover these expenses. As an alternative to buying an 'all-inclusive' funeral through an undertaker, some people have chosen, as far as possible, to make their own arrangements – for example, buying a coffin, asking friends to carry the coffin, and so on. This can be complex, but for those interested in so-called 'DIY' funerals there is a very full account in *The Natural Death Handbook*, edited by Nicholas Albery, Gil Elliot and Joseph Elliot of the Natural Death Centre.

3 In what ways can the funeral be made personally meaningful? It may be that a particular piece of music, or a hymn, or particular types of flowers, or a particular type of service may add to the meaning of the event. Some have found being intimately involved in the funeral arrangements a valuable way of making the funeral personally significant. Others have found a non-religious ceremony more acceptable than the traditional religious format. The British Humanist Association can provide a trained funeral officiant for approximately £60. Or a humanist service can be provided by anyone willing to officiate. The British Humanist Association offers guidance on how to conduct such services through a publication by Jane Wynne Willson, *Funerals Without God*. Their address is provided in Appendix 1.

The responsibilities of funeral directors
Giving attention to the details of a funeral may be a considerable strain on the bereaved person. But a helpful undertaker can make the process very much easier.

When consulting a funeral director is is advisable to discuss the services they provide in detail. Consider the options. For example, the funeral service can take place in a church or other place of worship, in a cemetery, chapel, the undertaker's chapel, or at the graveside itself. Personal preferences should be discussed; for example, if a particular piece of music is wanted (which could be live, or a recording), of if it is desired that a friend or relative speak at the service, or something be read that has some personal significance. In addition to considering various options about the service itself, it is advisable to look at the chapel, and to ask about arrangements for preparing and viewing the body. Preferences about how the body should be clothed, and whether make-up should be used in the preparation of the body should also be discussed. Some people prefer having the body in the family home until the funeral, others prefer the body to remain in the undertaker's chapel. Good funeral directors willingly discuss the options in a considerate and sensitive way. Any funeral director who does not show this care is best avoided.

It is advisable to consult several funeral directors and obtain written estimates stating exactly what is provided and the cost, as costs do vary. Funeral directors who are members of the National Association of Funeral Directors (NAFD) are guided by a national code of practice. The code stipulates that the funeral director must provide information on various services and costs; that is, they have a professional responsibility to inform enquirers about the more economical services, as well as the more expensive. Unfortunately not all funeral directors who claim to be members of the Association actually follow the code, so it is wise to consult several. (One study noted that 97% of customers only consult one funeral director.) Services available should range from a simple basic funeral that does not include things such as church or crematorium fees, flowers, the following car, or embalming, to more elaborate comprehensive services which include a wide range of additional features. When a funeral director who is a member of NAFD provides a written estimate for a particular service they are bound by their code of practice not to exceed the estimated cost without the customer's permission.

Burial
Burials can take place in churchyards or cemeteries, or even on private land. For information about costs and availability of space in a churchyard the priest or minister should be consulted. It is now more common to be buried in a cemetery as many churchyards are full. Cemeteries are run either by the local authority or a private company. Most cemeteries are non-denominational, although there may be specific areas allocated to particular faiths. Most types of service or ceremony can be conducted at a non-denominational cemetery. Once again the cost of grave space varies, so it is best to check several sites if a choice has not already been made. If it is desired that the burial should occur somewhere other than a churchyard or cemetery

permission will need to be obtained; once again a funeral director can offer guidance on this. To carry out their function funeral directors will want the Certificate for Burial or Cremation received from the Registrar, or an Order for Burial from the coroner.

Cremation
The paperwork needed for cremation is rather more complicated than that for burial. As noted above, cremation cannot occur before the cause of death is known for certain. There are five forms that have to be completed. An Application Form for cremation **(form A)** has to be signed by the next of kin or the executor. Two Cremation Certificates **(forms B and C)** which must be signed by two different doctors are required. There is a charge for these two. However, if the death has been referred to the coroner, he or she will provide a Certificate for Cremation, in which case the two Cremation Certificates are not needed. A Crematorium Certificate **(form F)** is signed by the medical referee at the crematorium. The medical referee can refuse to authorise the cremation and order a post-mortem or refer to the coroner. Finally, a **Certificate for Burial or Cremation** (which is issued by the Registrar) will be needed unless a coroner has issued a Certificate for Cremation. Forms A, B, C and F are available from the funeral director or crematorium. If there are any questions about these forms the funeral director will be able to help.

Making a Complaint
If the funeral director is a member of the National Association of Funeral Directors (NAFD) a formal complaint can be made by contacting the National Secretary of the NAFD; the address is given in Appendix 1. Advice about making a complaint concerning some aspect of the service or the bill can be obtained from the Citizens' Advice Bureau or the Trading Standards Department of the local council.

Summary

The practical matters that need to be attended to following a death can seem endless. This chapter has provided a simple outline, but things can be very much more complicated. For the bereaved person these matters can be a source of considerable stress, hence offers of practical assistance from relatives or friends will usually be welcomed and appreciated.

7 Helping people mourn

In this chapter I will use the term 'helper' to refer to a relative, friend or neighbour who has not received any specific training in helping people suffering bereavements. In the next chapter we will look at circumstances where trained help may be needed.

Despite the pain and difficulties of grief and mourning most people come to terms with their loss without requiring counselling or therapy. Research has consistently shown that a crucial factor determining intensity of grief and speed of recovery is the degree to which the mourner feels supported and helped by others. It was noted in chapter 2 that the extent to which a person is able to derive help and encouragement from their various relationships may be referred to as their level of 'social support'.

Most people are able to adapt to loss with social support from family, friends and neighbours. But it must also be noted that many bereaved people do not feel that they receive the level or type of help that is needed, and consequently have to struggle through on their own. Without help and support from others the experience of bereavement is often more painful, more traumatic, and more prolonged than it needs to be. But it would be wrong to assume that a lack of support from family, friends or neighbours means these people are indifferent towards the bereaved person's suffering. We turn away from another person's grief for many different reasons. Our own fears of death or loss, our own grief, or not knowing what to say or do, may lead us to avoid contact with someone we know has lost someone close to them. We feel unable to tolerate their pain, unable to respond to their grief. And yet the appearance of a person mourning the loss of a loved one often calls out for a caring response. The tears, the facial expression, the dejected posture, the evident suffering and visible distress, will often prompt a desire to help, to give some kind of assistance. As noted in the discussion of attachment behaviour in chapter 1 these behaviours are likely to evoke sympathy and a desire to help in others. But how should be respond? In the face of a mourner's grief, what can we say? What can we do? How can we help when, after all, we are powerless to give the sufferer what they so desperately want: the return of the person who has died?

There is now a substantial body of research which has sought to answer the central question: what do people who have been through the pain of losing a loved one find most helpful? Fortunately, on the basis of reports from people who have actually been through the process of mourning a major loss, some clear guidelines indicating what is, and what is not helpful have emerged.

We noted in chapter 1 that mourning is a process. It is a process that involves coming to terms with, or adapting to, loss. And we have seen this process can be described in various ways. Briefly reviewing this will help with the later discussion.

Bowlby describes the process of mourning in terms of Four Phases. During the initial phase of 'Numbness' or shock, the bereaved person may appear stunned, as if they are unable to respond to what has happened. The second phase, that of 'Yearning', often involves a desperate longing for the deceased; the mourner may literally search for them, and often display angry protest at their absence. A third phase, termed 'Disorganisation', is where the restless, agitated activity of the second phase gives way to withdrawal, sadness, and perhaps depression or despair. The fourth phase involves the gradual 'Reorganisation' of the mourner's life and of their sense of who they are, without the lost person.

Worden offers a different perspective, seeing the process of mourning in terms of Four Tasks. These Four Tasks are firstly, to recognise the loss is real and irreversible. Secondly, to experience and express the emotions provoked by the loss. Thirdly, to adapt to the changes brought by the loss. And fourthly, what can be seen as finally letting go of the attachment to the deceased as a person existing in the external world, and 'relocating' them, as it were, inside the self – in the mourner's inner world' – and moving on with life.

Bowlby and Worden emphasise that these descriptions are not blueprints. Individuals are different, they grieve and mourn differently. The Four Phases and Four Tasks are not presented as a series of distinct, clear-cut steps that a person must pass through, or accomplish in a prescribed order. They are not offered as rules that mourners must follow. The process of mourning is often too chaotic to be represented in terms of a neat scheme of distinct orderly steps. At any one time a mourner may experience aspects of several Phases, or be working on several Tasks. The idea of phases or tasks provides very useful guidelines to help us understand what the process of mourning involves, as long as we are careful not to apply them rigidly.

For the purpose of this chapter an essential point to bear in mind from these descriptions is that the process of mourning changes over time. A consequence of this is that different forms of help are needed at different times. What is a helpful response when someone has just heard of their loss may be very unhelpful some months later. What is helpful at one time may be unhelpful at another. In this chapter we will look at ways of helping the bereaved person work through the process of mourning. The focus will be on specific things a helper can do. Taken together, these suggestions – based mainly on accounts given by bereaved people themselves, offer a practical guide to how relatives, neighbours or friends, who have no formal training in working with the bereaved, can assist the process of mourning.

Encouraging the expression of feelings

Writing in the mid-1960s Geoffrey Gorer observed: 'Giving way to grief is stigmatised as morbid, unhealthy, demoralising. The proper action of a friend and well-wisher is felt to be distraction of a mourner from his or her grief'. Unfortunately the situation does not appear to have changed dramatically since then. Bereaved people continue to describe experiences of doubtlessly well-intentioned relatives, friends, or neighbours, trying to stop them crying, or prevent them talking about their loss, or in some other way trying to distract them from their grief. As Gorer notes, one reason why people do this is because of the belief that indulging grief, 'letting yourself go' and really experiencing the pain, is unhealthy, unnecessary, or even dangerous. The belief is that someone who really allows themselves to feel sorrow will make the situation worse, perhaps bringing on a deep depression or even make themselves feel suicidal. This is still a very common view, but it is very mistaken. It is an aspect of our attitude to suffering. The ancient idea that in certain circumstances suffering can be healing, that suffering can in some sense be 'redemptive' is very unfashionable in 'developed' societies. But if the idea that suffering is always to be averted leads us to avoid the pain of grief, the process of mourning will be interrupted and prolonged. This is one of the ways in which culture can interfere with mourning. But the belief that grief or suffering is always bad is not the only reason why well-wishers often try to distract mourners from their grief.

A second reason is that in distracting the mourner we distract ourselves. As noted in our discussion of attachment behaviour, someone suffering bereavement will display behaviours that will often provoke a desire to help in others. This desire to help is, in large measure, due to the fact that witnessing the distress of the bereaved is distressing to the observer. Hence, if we can reduce the distress in the bereaved, we can reduce our own distress. A person in mourning, particularly during the phases of 'Yearning' and 'Disorganisation', may cry, call out for the lost person, and be so distressed they may appear helpless and unable to manage everyday affairs. In such a condition the mourner's thoughts and feelings will be taken up with their loss, longing for the return of their loved one. They may be unable to focus on other things, and unable to respond to others. We are dealing with powerful feelings that can seem to be unmanageable. For both the mourner and the helper there may be real fears that the distress and panic will never end, that the grief will overwhelm them. The grief may be so intense that the sufferer fears they will not be able to survive it, that they will go mad or die themselves. A helper may have similar anxieties about the condition of the mourner. But they may also fear the intensity of the feelings being aroused in themselves. It is not easy to witness desperation and pain in others, and it is not easy to contain the feelings which someone else's pain evokes in us. (In practice it is in fact very difficult to disentangle the two.) A helper may experience deeply disturbing feelings which can easily interfere with their response to the mourner. Loss is both painful and universal, hence a helper faced with a mourner's grief must cope with the suffering of the other person, and what witnessing such suffering provokes in themselves. The desire to distract the mourner from their grief may reflect a need to contain the helper's own feelings of loss.

Instead of trying to distract a mourner from their grief it is likely to be much more helpful if they are allowed, or even encouraged, to experience and express the pain of their loss. Repeatedly, the accounts given by people who have experienced major bereavements make it clear that where the response from others suggests that they cannot tolerate the mourner's distress and hence try to distract them, the mourner is left feeling isolated, with their grief experienced as an unmanageable burden. Whereas in situations where others accept the expression of pain and distress the mourner feels supported and encouraged.

Although it is generally agreed by workers in this field that crying is helpful to the mourner, there are many cultural restrictions limiting where, when, and who can or should cry. The pressure to 'put on a brave face', and 'bottle up' feelings, is often very strong, and is yet another way in which social conventions can serve to exacerbate grief. Many bereaved people report holding back their tears out of concern for others, not wanting to upset other people. As a result mourners often try to suppress their tears. Men often feel under great pressure to control their feelings and, as they see it, 'be strong' and 'manly'.

Anger is an emotion that is frequently felt after a major loss, and it is often a feeling that presents difficulties for helpers. Bowlby notes that during the 'Yearning' phase of mourning in particular, the bereaved person may display angry protest against their loss. Relatives, friends and neighbours of a bereaved person may find it difficult to be with them when they are experiencing these feelings, as the feelings may well be expressed through rejection or hostility towards anyone who offers help. This can be very confusing: on the one hand the mourner may show themself to be in evident distress, and show signs of needing support and assistance, but on the other hand may reject offers of help. If offers of help are rejected it is natural to want to withdraw from the mourner in some way. If the mourner is being critical of the helper or someone else, the helper may want to defend themself or the other person. But withdrawing, contradicting or arguing with the mourner is unlikely to be helpful. Although there can be many reasons for the mourner's anger, one initial factor may be that they are struggling against accepting the reality of the loss, perhaps desperately looking for evidence that there has been a mistake. Anyone who acknowledges their loss in effect reminds them of the reality of what has happened. The helper reinforces the truth that the mourner desperately wants to deny: that their loved one has died and will not return. At such times it is not so much what is said that is helpful. The presence of someone who cares, and who is willing to accept the mourner's anger, distress and confusion, without taking offence, retaliating, trying to distract them, or pretending everything is fine, or will be fine, is usually very helpful (even though it may not appear to be so at the time).

Following the turmoil of these agitated, desperate and confusing emotions, mourners often experience a period of withdrawal, depression, and even despair. Bowlby refers to this as the phase of 'Disorganisation'. The mourner may lack motivation for even the most basic tasks of caring for themselves or their home. They may be uncommunicative and unconsolable. A helper may feel that they must try to cheer them up, or cajole them into being more active. But once again some degree of withdrawal, often accompanied by depression, is a natural feature of mourning and should not cause alarm.

It is important to recognise the need for repetition, for going over the same ground repeatedly. For example, the first Task of Mourning involves accepting the loss has occurred, and that it is real and irreversible. This may take time, and the mourner may need to 'discover' the reality of their loss in different ways. As Worden notes, this is a task, it requires effort, and often involves struggle. The mourner may strongly resist recognising that the loss is real. They may go over and over the circumstances of the death, perhaps in an effort to discover that some mistake has occurred, that the person has not really died. It will not help the bereaved person if others try to distract them from this. For many mourners the repetition is necessary. Similarly, the second Task of Mourning, which involves working through the pain of loss, usually entails much repetition, and hence takes time. Trying to get the mourner to focus on something else, look to the future, get busy or involved in something, feel better or cheer up, is unlikely to be helpful. For the same reason the use of tranquillisers or alcohol to deaden the pain is unlikely to be helpful.

To summarise this section we can note that to be helpful it is important to remember two points. Firstly, that the distress and turmoil associated with grief are natural and will pass in time. And secondly, it is far better to express pain and sorrow, repeatedly if necessary, than to suppress it.

Physical contact

One way that a bereaved person can be encouraged to express their feelings is through physical contact. The following experience was described by Sylvia, whose husband was killed in a road accident when he was returning from a business trip.

> I was at home on Friday evening, early in December, drinking coffee, and chatting to Ann, my neighbour. The door bell rang and at the door was a policeman. Obviously you know straight away that something is wrong. 'Mrs. Stevens?' My heart sank. I said: 'Yes. What's wrong?' He looked down and said: 'I'm sorry to have to bring you some bad news, can I come in?' We went into the kitchen. Afterwards Ann said I had turned pale and already seemed in a state of shock. Then the policeman said: 'It's your husband...'. After that I went blank. Ann showed the policeman to the door. I remember standing in the kitchen, stunned, unable to think, feel or do anything. Ann was standing close by, she said something but I can't remember what. Ann reached towards me and the moment her hand touched my shoulder I burst into tears. Ann hugged me and I cried for what seemed to be hours....

Notice what Ann said and did. When Sylvia described this experience, she spoke very appreciatively of Ann's response. In particular Sylvia remembered two things that she found especially helpful. First, Ann said very little. And secondly, she put her arm around her and held her while she cried. As Sylvia noted: 'The hug said far more than words'. We may recall that for many people the first reaction to hearing about the death of a loved one, especially where the death is unexpected (as it was for Sylvia), is shock and numbness. The bereaved person seems to cut out much of what is happening around them as if they are unable to take in anything more. Much of what is said at such times is unlikely to be heard, or unlikely to register. Ann said very little, her desire to support and comfort her friend was shown mainly through physical contact. And notice that the physical contact didn't prevent the expression of emotion, it encouraged it. It was as if Ann was saying to Sylvia: 'It's all right to be upset, you don't need to hold back'. This 'permission' helped Sylvia to express her feelings and feel supported in doing so.

There is no doubt that the sort of contact described here can be experienced as helpful and supportive. But this is not always the case. There any many unspoken social rules specifying what is and what is not appropriate physical contact. Who we touch, how, when, where and for how long, are all regulated by elaborate social rules. We may not be able to list all these in detail, but the way we react when one of these restrictions is over-stepped reveals that we 'know' the rule well enough to feel discomfort when it is broken. Of course different societies, different cultures, have different rules defining what is, and what is not, acceptable physical contact. Clearly it is important to be aware of this, especially in a very mobile and multi-cultural society where relationships may be formed with people from a wide range of backgrounds. What we find comforting someone else may find offensive. Many things can be communicated by touch, and of course communication can be misinterpreted or misunderstood. A handshake can convey an ordinary greeting, but a handshake in which the hand is held for a slightly longer period than expected conveys something more; the handshake is more than a polite greeting, it has more significance, a more personal meaning. A man touching a woman he is not related to on the forearm may be reassuring; by contrast touching her hand may convey a sexual message. The description of the contact between Ann and Sylvia may seem perfectly ordinary, perfectly appropriate. But how would it appear if instead I had described two men? Or what if Sylvia had been with a male friend, or a male relative (a brother, for example)? Or what if the man had been twice her age, or half her age? What if he was her best friend's husband, or a new neighbour? Would it have been appropriate for the policeman to respond in the same way as Ann? What if Sylvia and Ann had only recently met? What if they were new neighbours and Sylvia was of Pakistani origin, or West Indian? How do these factors change the situation? Do you think Ann would have been comforted or made uncomfortable? The nature of the relationship alters what is and is not appropriate physical contact even in this situation.

Women are perhaps more at ease providing and accepting the sort of physical comfort that came so naturally to Ann and that Sylvia found so helpful. For many men physical contact with other men is more extensively controlled by social conventions. For example, men can touch other men if they are a team member who scores a goal, but outside such clearly defined situations physical contact between men is subject to a powerful taboo. Just as many men are reluctant to express grief in front of others, they may be very inhibited in showing supportive warmth in the spontaneous way that Ann did. Of course not all men conform to such oppressive social norms but powerful restrictions remain operative for many men. These restrictions provide another example of how cultural factors can add to the burden of grief, and can be an obstacle in the way of providing, and receiving, help.

Given the wide variety of relationships, individual preferences, the complexity of social rules, and the possibility of misinterpretation, it is not possible to specify what type of physical contact is going to be experienced as comforting and supportive. But we should not underestimate how significant touch is in these situations and, as long as we are careful not to make the mourner uncomfortable, it can be greatly appreciated. Even a light touch on the arm can convey warmth and support. As a general guide it can be said that very few people would resent all physical contact when they are in distress. A tentative move towards some form of physical contact allows the mourner to respond, and our sensitivity to this response can guide us as to what is appropriate.

Listening and talking

We have noted that the process of mourning can be described in terms of Four Tasks. These Tasks describe the process of adapting to loss, and each Task involves effort and takes time. When offering support to someone who is bereaved it is important to remember that work on each of the Four Tasks will need to be done repeatedly. Going over the circumstances of the loss, reviewing the past, and talking about the changes that have occurred since the death, are all necessary features of mourning. Throughout the process of mourning the bereaved person can be helped by having someone listen. A helper can help simply by being available to listen, perhaps asking questions about the deceased and the past. This helps make the loss real – reinforcing the painful truth that the loss is irreversible. However, a helper can become impatient if they have heard the mourner talk about some aspect of their loss many times before. A helper may need to remind themselves that such repetition is valuable; it is an essential part of adapting to the loss. Listening to and encouraging such talk facilitates the process of mourning. A helper may feel it is time the mourner looked to the future and let go of the past. But once again it must be emphasised that people differ in the speed with which they adapt to loss. It is important that the mourner is able to come to terms with their loss in their own time.

Often relatives, neighbours or friends who would like to help avoid the mourner because they don't know what to say. Much of this reluctance appears to be related to beliefs such as: 'I must be careful not to upset them. It would be awful if they started to cry'. Or, 'I must make them feel better'. As we have seen, such ideas are mistaken and very unhelpful. The role of a helper is not to take away a mourner's grief. A mourner needs to accept the reality of their loss, and experience the feelings provoked by the loss. A few words can often facilitate this process. A few words can either encourage the expression of feeling, or block such expression. Asking 'How do you feel today?' invites a focus on feelings. Similarly the mourner can be encouraged in their remembering, their review of the past they have shared with the deceased, by simple questions. But of course if such prompts are not picked up, the mourner may not at that time wish to focus on these issues. There is no need to push the point. A helper can help by inviting the mourner to express their thoughts and feelings about their loss. It remains the mourner's choice whether they take up the invitation.

In an effort to avoid upsetting the bereaved person, relatives, friends and neighbours may try to steer the conversation away from anything associated with death or loss. They may try to avoid talking about the deceased, not even mentioning their name. Once again this is a very common aspect of conventional behaviour that actually inhibits the process of mourning. Bereaved people are often extremely sensitive to the way their loss can become an embarrassment to others. They may stop talking about the deceased and try to put the past behind them. But this will tend to isolate them, and prevent completion of the tasks of mourning.

At times, especially during the phase of 'Disorganisation', relatives, friends and neighbours may think the bereaved person has 'let themselves go' or 'are going downhill'. The helper may feel like saying: 'You must snap out of it. It's no good feeling sorry for yourself, life has to go on'. Needless to say such comments are unlikely to be helpful. But equally unhelpful are what has been termed 'clichés of comfort'. These are stereotyped remarks aimed at offering comfort or support, but which generally have the opposite effect. Tom lost his wife when he was sixty-two. He had many friends who rallied round to help and offer support. But he was bombarded with statements such as: 'She had a good innings', 'Don't worry, you will get over it', 'At least she's not suffering now', 'She wouldn't be happy to see you so depressed', 'She's gone to a better place'. These and similar statements were experienced by Tom as very dismissive of his grief: 'All those words. They didn't mean anything. No-one wanted to notice how much I hurt'.

The belief that we must 'not speak ill of the dead' is very common, and can be a source of guilt as well as inhibition. The bereaved person may feel intense guilt because they are angry with the person they have lost. But accepting negative feelings can be a great relief. There are negative feelings in the very best of relationships. Complaints against our closest family and friends are perfectly natural. Just acknowledging that everyone feels annoyance with, as well as love for, those they are closest to, that there is nothing in this to be guilty about, and no reason to feel we need to conceal our feelings, is often helpful. Initially there may be a tendency to deny any negative feelings and paint an unrealistic, or idealised, picture of the deceased. Mavis lost her husband after fifty-two years of marriage. She repeatedly claimed: 'He was the best man in the world'. But this idealistic picture gave way, after fifteen months, to: 'He was a wonderful man – but he could be a sod at times'. This is a very important shift; being able to describe the lost person realistically without exaggerating their positive or negative sides is an achievement of working through the complex and often muddled feelings evoked by loss.

Acknowledging and accepting the mourner's anger, regardless of where it is directed, is likely to be experienced as supportive. This does not mean you have to agree with complaints; the important thing is to see the expression of anger as a necessary aspect of the second Task of Mourning: working through the pain of loss. Allowing the tears to flow, and the anger to be expressed, will ultimately lead to healing. Being prepared to listen to whatever the mourner needs to express is an important way of offering care and support.

Avoiding offering advice

It is often assumed that some change in the bereaved person's circumstances would help them get over their loss more easily. Mourners may be advised, by well-meaning relatives, friends or neighbours, to take a long holiday, go and stay with a relative, move house, or even get married. Some bereaved people do make dramatic changes in their life as a quite deliberate way of distancing themselves from their loss, doing this without any encouragement from others. But other bereaved people describe being persuaded by others to make some change because they 'will feel much better'.

However, if the motive for, and the result of, such changes is to get away from grief it is unlikely to be helpful. Any attempt to resist recognising the reality of the loss, and the pain that arises with that recognition, will probably delay adapting to the loss rather than be helpful. It is undoubtedly true that some mourners find taking a holiday, or going to stay with relatives or friends helpful. But the general principle is that any such change will only be helpful in the long run if it does not block or interrupt the process of mourning. Staying with a relative or friend can be helpful as long as the bereaved person is not actively distracted from their mourning.

Dorothy, a sixty-year-old widow, went to stay with her sister in Canada soon after the loss of her husband Bill. The problem with her visit, which lasted several months, was that her sister Violet felt it was her duty to help Dorothy forget her loss, put the past behind her, and get on with making a 'new future'.

Attempts to cheer her up, and even some desperate attempts at match-making, may have been well-intentioned, but were in fact decidedly unhelpful. Dorothy had to cut short her stay and return to England to, as she said, 'be alone with my memories'.

It may be very helpful, and greatly appreciated, if invitations are extended to the bereaved. But offering advice such as: 'You must get away for a while', 'You ought to go and stay with your sister', 'You should sell the house and move closer to your brother', 'You have to look to the future', 'You should buy yourself a new set of clothes and look for another partner', is unlikely to be helpful.

Acceptance and reassurance

Sometimes bereaved people are disturbed not only by their loss but also by their own reactions. In chapter 1 it was noted that some aspects of grief can appear quite bizarre. The bereaved person may refuse to sleep in their bed, or they may insist on setting out a place at mealtimes for the deceased, or say they talk to the deceased, or that they actually see them. Such experiences may make the mourner feel they are going mad, or losing control or perhaps even dying themselves. But these experiences should not cause alarm. If the bereaved person can see that they are not being regarded as odd, abnormal or crazy when the describe these experiences, and that the listener is not surprised or disturbed, and doesn't tell them to take some tablets or go and see a doctor, this can be very reassuring. It can be very helpful to gently reassure the bereaved person that these experiences do not mean that there is something wrong with them, and that they are in fact normal responses to loss. It is often not necessary to say very much. Mourners are frequently very sensitive to how others respond to them, hence a great deal can be conveyed with few words and an attentive manner. But note that some bereaved people find these experiences satisfying. For some a sense of the presence of the deceased, or even hearing their voice, may be very comforting and they may not want such experiences to stop. Where this is the case it may be more helpful to simply acknowledge that these are common and form part of a natural process.

Helpers may benefit from reading through the sections on

the various aspects of grief and mourning in chapter 1, and the experiences described in chapters 3 and 4 in particular noticing the wide range of normal reactions to loss. Because deaths are comparatively rare, and people more isolated, there is much less common knowledge of what is involved in mourning. This lack of knowledge often breeds fear and increased isolation. Helpers can play an important role in 'normalising' the experiences of grief and mourning. That is, noting that strange or upsetting dreams, hallucinations, searching, talking to pictures, and many other common features of grief are normal and natural responses to loss. Furthermore, it is important to note that these aspects of grief can continue for many months, and perhaps for several years.

Offering practical assistance

As we have seen in chapter 6, the initial period following a loss may require the mourner to attend to various practical issues such as funeral arrangements, registering the death, dealing with financial matters, and sorting out paperwork. The mourner may go through all of these procedures in a state of shock. It can be very helpful for the mourner if some assistance is offered with these tasks. For some the reality of the loss only really sinks in when the body is seen, or perhaps when the funeral arrangements are made. Accompanying a person to see the body, or helping them with funeral arrangements, can be very supportive and helpful, even though at the time the mourner may be too distressed to appreciate the help.

It appears from research that has been carried out in this field that help is most likely to be provided during the early stages of mourning. Such assistance is of course to be encouraged. However, many bereaved people report a very rapid decline in offers of practical help once the funeral is over. Ron was sixty when his wife Alice died. He had done hard physical work all his life and struggled to provide for their four sons. Immediately after Alice's death the four sons and their families were frequent visitors to Ron's home, offering help, listening and talking. But Ron's anger with the staff at the hospital where Alice died made it very difficult for him to respond to the family's help. About three months after Alice's death Ron found himself alone in his home having had no contact with family, friends or neighbours for two weeks. Although Ron could understand why the visits had stopped he nonetheless felt isolated and rejected by all the people who had been so supportive in the early days of his loss.

Ron's experience is only too common and is very unfortunate, as family, friends and neighbours can do much to help the bereaved person cope with the process of mourning that necessarily extends far beyond the time of the funeral. In particular during the phase of mourning termed 'Disorganisation', the mourner may neglect housework and self-care. Offering practical assistance, perhaps doing some shopping or helping with household chores, may be especially valuable during this phase. However, the problem with this sort of help is that it can become a routine that the mourner comes to rely on. This can then become, in the long run, an obstacle to working on the third Task of Mourning, adjusting to a new life without the deceased.

Lee requested help with depression. She was twenty and studying for a degree in history. Her parents had come to England from Jamaica thirty years ago. Her father had died when she was twelve. Since then Lee and her two elder sisters had cared for her mother, but after her sisters married and left home, Lee took responsibility for caring for the household and dealing with finances. Lee felt a strong sense of duty towards her mother and was very diligent in carrying out the obligations she took upon herself. Unfortunately she was not able to continue her degree and part-time job as well as managing the housework and care of her mother. Part of the difficulty was that her mother was quite understandably anxious at the prospect of being left alone if all of her daughters should leave home and marry. Over the years Lee's mother had allowed the comfort and support of her daughters to become indispensable, and she found the prospect of losing this help intolerable. The experience of Lee and her family illustrates how long-term problems can develop if a bereaved person becomes unnecessarily dependent on practical help from others.

Staying in touch

We have noted that physical contact can be very supportive and helpful. But staying in touch, keeping up contact, in the sense of continued communication is also very important. Many bereaved people describe receiving much needed help and support in the period immediately after their loss, but soon afterwards contact with relatives, friends or neighbours may seem to evaporate. Often mourners feel they are expected to have recovered and be 'back to normal' within a few weeks of the death. But as we have seen the process of mourning can often take many months, or even several years, to complete. Over this period a common pattern is for the mourner to experience successive 'highs' and 'lows'. Periods of feeling they are coping well with their loss and getting on with life will be followed by a return of feelings of anxiety or depression, and a sense of having slipped back. Contact with others is often given as the main factor in helping mourners cope with recurring feelings of despondency and apprehension. But many bereaved people find they experience periods when they lack the will and energy to maintain contact with others. Hence relatives, friends and neighbours usually need to take the initiative to remain in contact with the mourner. There are simple ways of staying in touch and these can be very supportive. A phone call, a card or letter, a few words, a brief visit, or even a wave when meeting by chance, can make a difference. It is striking how often bereaved people describe such apparently small gestures as significant events in the process of recovery from loss. Mourners remember such gestures, and value them, long after their mourning has passed.

Elizabeth, a fifty-six-year-old widow, described how moved she was when she received a postcard from a friend who was away on holiday. The note was brief but included the simple words 'Thinking of you'. For Elizabeth this meant that despite her difficulties coming to terms with her loss, and all the time she had felt unable to respond to the efforts of well-wishers, she had not been abandoned. People still cared. The concern of other people helped her survive, and small gestures of kindness and consideration helped her through a very difficult period of mourning. It is important not to underestimate the value to the bereaved person of even apparently small acts of thoughtfulness and kindness that demonstrate care and concern.

Recreating social life

'Reorganisation', the fourth Phase of Mourning, involves the gradual reconstruction of the mourner's life without the lost person. This process of rebuilding is described by Worden as Task Three and Four: to adjust to an environment in which the deceased is missing; and to emotionally relocate the deceased and move on with life. The bereaved person gradually adapts to life without the deceased. This often involves learning new skills and taking on new roles. The process includes learning how to engage with life and other people on a new footing. As well as coming to terms with the changes the loss has brought externally, the mourner must come to terms with the loss inside themselves. What Worden calls 'relocating' the deceased refers to the need for the mourner to find a place for the deceased in their emotional life that allows them to go on and rebuild their life. This will require seeing themselves and the world differently. It is not just their life that needs to be reorganised, it is their identity – their sense of who they are.

Relatives, friends and neighbours can often give important assistance during this period. 'Reorganisation' often involves re-establishing contacts and relationships that may have been neglected during a period of 'Disorganisation' and withdrawal that may have continued for a year or more. However, many bereaved people form new relationships altogether. This process may be full of uncertainty and anxiety. Relatives, friends and neighbours can help by extending invitations and offering opportunities to the bereaved person to re-establish social contacts. However, it may be that the mourner does not want to re-associate with a group of people that they felt connected to only through the deceased. They may have socialised with others largely as the partner of the deceased. Just as their loss changes their identity, it changes their relationships. It is in fact very common for bereaved people to break associations with one group – perhaps the relatives of the deceased – and build new associations in a different group. Sandra, for example, had been devoted to her husband Ray. She had made many sacrifices in order to help him develop a furniture business he had begun soon after their marriage. As the years passed Sandra had lost contact with old friends and rarely saw her family. Her social life centred around being 'Ray's wife'. After Ray's death from lung cancer Sandra found herself at thirty-two without knowing anyone for whom she was not 'Ray's widow'. For Sandra 'Reorganisation' involved establishing a new network of friendships that were formed on the basis of her own personal choice, and that saw her as an individual in her own right, rather than, as she felt she had become, an appendage to someone else.

Being available

The helper essentially needs to be available; not to force the mourner to face their loss, but to be available as a support when they do. It has been repeatedly emphasised in this book that there is no fixed pattern, no blueprint, or set of rules stipulating how the process of mourning should proceed. Everyone is different; people adjust to loss in different ways, and at different rates. The most we can have are guidelines which are general descriptions of what appear to be the most significant aspects of the process, based on many observations. The general nature of these descriptions should not be forgotten. It will not help if a relative, friend or neighbour decides that it is about time the bereaved person moved on to the third Task of Mourning as they have already spent six weeks on the second Task! This would be a serious misunderstanding of the notion of Tasks of Mourning, and certainly would not help the mourner. Being available involves acknowledging the personal nature of grief, and being willing to offer support and assistance as the mourner struggles with their loss in their own way.

The process of mourning may take years to work through. A helper can offer recognition of the magnitude of the loss and the pain of grief, and permit the mourner to express their pain in words and tears again and again, simply by being present. It is important not to shun the person, or try to avoid their pain, which also in practice means not avoiding our own pain. Allowing the mourner space to grieve, tolerating the distress and repetition without trying to block the process, and not taking offence when the mourner, as very often happens, appears oblivious or ungrateful, are all aspects of 'being available'. Essentially it is being available emotionally which is the most important aspect of 'availability'. 'Being with' the mourner, being available, can be a subtle process, beyond words. There can be no rules governing what to say and do in these situations, but a desire to help and respond appropriately, and a willingness to follow the mourner, will help in providing what is needed.

Summary

The guidelines offered in this chapter are based largely on accounts from bereaved people themselves. Offering help and support to the bereaved is mainly a matter of demonstrating care and concern for them. It is not a matter of 'saying the right thing' or knowing a great deal about bereavement. The crucial thing is to show concern and a willingness to help. It is also worth remembering that support from others – family, friends and neighbours – is the single most significant factor influencing the outcome of mourning. The value of help and support from others, where the mourner is allowed to face their loss and express their feelings, cannot be overestimated.

8 Befriending, counselling and therapy

Befriending, counselling and therapy are all sources of help that may be available in addition to the support that may be offered by family, friends and neighbours. In this chapter we will first consider situations where counselling or therapy may be needed, and then look at the increasing availability of 'befriending'.

Complicated mourning

Most people manage to cope with the painful process of mourning without help from counsellors or therapists. However, it appears that about a third of people experiencing a major bereavement do require some form of counselling or therapy. In order to identify who may benefit from trained help the term 'complicated mourning' has been used to refer to a number of conditions that are likely to require the assistance of a counsellor or therapist. The Oxford English Dictionary defines 'complication' as 'involved condition; entangled state of affairs; complicating circumstances; secondary disease or condition aggravating a previous one'. This seems to describe the situation we are considering reasonably well. That is, there are some situations in which the process of adapting to loss is made particularly difficult because of various aggravating factors. Later in this chapter we will consider some of these aggravating, or complicating factors. There are other terms used to refer to these difficulties; for example, 'unresolved' grief or mourning. However, I will use the term 'complicated' to preserve the analogy, used throughout this book, between a major loss and a physical injury.

In chapter 1 we considered the wide range of responses that may be experienced after a significant loss: these can include sadness, depression, anxiety, anger, resentment, guilt, tearfulness, hallucinations of the deceased, dreams of the deceased, and sensing the presence of the deceased. All of these responses are normal, common features of bereavement. They can all be regarded as features of uncomplicated grief, or uncomplicated mourning. Furthermore, we noted that mourning is a process involving a number of features which can be considered from various perspectives, such as in terms of phases or tasks. There are times, however, when it is apparent that the process of mourning has been disrupted in some way. The essential feature of complicated mourning is that the process of mourning is interrupted or blocked, and the mourner is unable to work through the process to an adequate completion. The bereaved person is unable to adjust to their loss, and in particular unable to work through the grief arising from that loss. We can identify four general types of complicated mourning: delayed grief, disguised grief, prolonged grief and exaggerated grief. We can consider each of these forms of complicated mourning as different ways of becoming stuck in the earlier phases of mourning. The bereaved person is unable to move on towards what Bowlby calls the phase of 'Reorganisation', or accomplish what Worden describes as the third and fourth Tasks of Mourning: adjusting to the changes brought about by the loss, emotionally relocating the deceased, and moving on with life. The various details of complicated mourning have been described in a number of ways; we will consider each in turn:

Delayed grief
A very common initial response to loss is disbelief. 'This can't be happening, there must be some mistake', expresses a hope that the loss is not real. Hoping that the death has not really occurred may persist for days. There may be an absence of grief, or there may be some grief but conspicuously less than would be expected considering the significance of the loss. The loss of a partner, a child, or a parent in childhood, are examples of major bereavements where generally we would expect considerable distress and pain. It is not uncommon for the shock of a major loss, or the first phase of mourning termed 'Numbness', to result in a delay in the experience of grief. This can be understood as a form of self-protection, a period where grief is temporarily kept at bay. But with some people the absence of grief persists. However, again we must be careful. Although some people may show little emotion because they are in a state of shock, it may

be the case that they simply do not respond in an emotional way. Recent research with widows and widowers suggests that between a quarter and two thirds are not greatly distressed by their loss, and yet show no evidence of 'complications'. This research finding needs to be borne in mind especially when wondering if the relative absence of emotions indicates a disruption of the mourning process. Relatively low levels of emotional experience or expression do not necessarily indicate complicated mourning. It is important to remember that individuals respond very differently to loss: some people are more emotional, or less inhibited in expressing emotions than others. Furthermore, some mourners describe consciously deciding to hold back their tears deliberately, or avoid their grief temporarily. However, delayed grief as a form of complicated mourning can reveal itself in many ways. It may happen that a person experiences little or no grief in relation to a major loss, but reacts intensely at a later date to a minor loss. Sometimes the mourner may say they accept the loss but continually avoid reminders of the deceased. For example, they may be unable to look at pictures of the deceased, or listen to music associated with the deceased. These are other forms of avoidance serve to keep the experience of grief at bay, either partly, or in some cases, completely. Work on the second Task of Mourning, working through the pain of loss, appears to be indefinitely postponed.

Phyllis was sixty-eight when she lost her son David. He was a builder and died after falling from a scaffold. David was divorced and lived alone but visited his mother every Wednesday evening, when he would do jobs around her home and she would cook them a meal and provide him with clean ironed shirts. Two years after the loss, Phyllis continued washing and ironing David's shirts and setting his place for a meal every Wednesday evening. Although in one sense Phyllis knew David was dead and they would never share an evening together again, part of her simply could not believe he was gone and would never return. It was as if continuing her Wednesday evening routine allowed her to hold on to the idea that one day he would return. In terms of the Four Tasks of Mourning Phyllis appeared to be stuck at the first Task: she was having difficulty accepting the reality of the loss.

Disguised grief

There are many ways in which grief can be disguised, or as some prefer to term it 'masked'. Grief that is not felt or expressed at the time of a loss can show itself in various ways at a later date. Unacknowledged or unexpressed grief can make itself felt in the form of physical symptoms, for example, physical pains. Sometimes the physical complaint of the bereaved person reflects the cause of death of the person they have lost. Harold's father died of a heart attack soon after he had been told he had stomach cancer. At the time of his father's death Harold was very busy changing his job and moving house. He remembered 'being in a daze' at the funeral and for some time afterwards. It was as if he had become stuck in the first Phase of Mourning, that of 'Numbness'. Six years after his father's death Harold developed severe stomach and chest pains for which no physical cause could be found despite extensive investigations. Therapy provided Harold with an opportunity to experience and express his deep sense of loss and grief at his father's death. He was able to face his feelings of guilt about being too busy to help his father in the period before he died, and being too busy to help the family in the months after the death. It was as if Harold's physical pains eventually forced him to pay attention to his feelings about his loss, and hence work on the second Task of Mourning: working through the pain of grief.

Various psychological difficulties, such as anxiety, phobias and depression, can be associated with disguised grief. One form of disguised grief that appears to be fairly common when a bereavement occurs in childhood or adolescence is recklessness or various forms of risk-taking – for example, drug abuse, dangerous driving, crime, and in some cases destructive and violent behaviour. Unfortunately at the time they occur such behaviours are often not recognised for what they are. A central feature of disguised grief is that the bereaved person generally does not see the link between the symptoms they suffer from and the unacknowledged or unexpressed grief.

Prolonged grief

Sometimes the experience of grief can be prolonged, the period of grief and mourning becomes excessive and mourning becomes chronic. Any of the features of grief described in chapter 1 can become a problem when they are experienced for an extended period. The difficulty, of course, is in specifying at what point grief and mourning should be regarded as being of excessive duration. As time passes grief usually recedes, the 'pangs of grief' become briefer, less frequent and less intense. It is often said that, as a general guide, if grief persists unabated beyond one year, trained help should be sought. But it is important to remember that some features of uncomplicated mourning can continue for many years; in particular anniversaries (of the death, or other important days like the deceased's birthday or wedding anniversary) can provoke renewed grief for many years after the death. The key word in the general guide suggested here is 'unabated'. If the grief is every bit as intense a year after the loss, some help may be needed. I should stress that this is a very general guide – some writers would argue for earlier intervention, some for later. Very often the bereaved person themselves will have a sense of being stuck, they will realise that they are 'not coming out of it', that for some reason they are not able to get beyond their grief.

Carl and Suzanne were on their honeymoon when they were involved in a car accident. Carl was seriously injured but survived. Unfortunately Suzanne died from her injuries. Carl described himself as 'going downhill' from that time on. He lost his job, and his friends and family gradually stopped associating with him. He experienced a wide range of common responses to loss: depression, tearfulness, anger, resentment, guilt, disturbed sleep, preoccupation with the circumstances of the accident, and the feeling that his life had lost meaning. But, after three years, Carl decided to seek help: 'I realised the way I was going I would never get over it. It was becoming worse the longer it went on. I tried to numb the pain with drink, but that didn't really help. Whatever I did I just sank deeper. I just couldn't pull myself out of it. I started to think it would only end when I joined Suzanne in the grave. That's when I came for help'. Carl expressed very vividly the sense of being stuck, or trapped in grief, of being unable to wrench free of it, or get beyond it. Carl came to realize in therapy that in a sense his grief was his connection to Suzanne and that by keeping hold of his grief he was, in a sense, keeping hold of Suzanne. Underlying his grief was an idea that if his grief went then Suzanne would also finally be gone.

This in fact is not an unusual form of complicated mourning.

A similar idea that is perhaps even more common is that grief is an expression of love or loyalty, and that if grief passes then love or loyalty has somehow come to an end or been reduced. The mourner may not be conscious of these ideas but they are, as it were, in the background, fuelling the grief. Such ideas can interfere with work on the second Task of Mourning: working through the pain of grief means experiencing the grief to the full and then moving beyond it.

Exaggerated grief

Any of the responses to loss described in chapter 1 can be experienced in an extreme form, to the point of disabling the mourner. For example, while sadness, and even depression, commonly occurs after bereavement this usually passes as the mourner begins to rebuild their life. In some cases, however, the depression can be so intense that the person is unable to function. Rather than being a feature of the general pattern of grief it's as if the depression 'takes over' as the central reaction to loss. Once again the bereaved person themself will often sense that they are stuck and are simply not able to work through the grief and adapt to the loss. In particular the phases of 'Yearning' and 'Disorganisation', and the first and second Tasks of Mourning can involve a wide range of feelings, any of which can be experienced in an exaggerated and disabling form.

A bereavement also frequently puts us in touch with our own fears of dying. These feelings usually diminish as the process of mourning progresses, but the fear of death can become a paralysing phobic response (thanatophobia) with panic attacks occurring persistently over a long period. This was the experience of Lynn, who was twenty when both of her parents died in a plane crash. Of course it is not surprising that such a tragedy should provoke intense grief and require a considerable period of time to adapt to the loss. But within weeks of the loss Lynn began having nightmares of being in a plane crash herself. Soon after this she started experiencing panic attacks whenever she thought about death. Lynn was unable to continue her university course and was unemployed for eight months before seeking help. Where any feature of the normal grief response is experienced in a severe and disabling form, it is advisable to seek trained help, through a GP or one of the organisations listed in Appendix 1.

Mourning is a process in which the mourner comes to accept what has happened, experiences feelings associated with the loss, and starts to rebuild their life without the deceased. People do this by degrees, and in their own way. Some will take longer than others to accept their loss and adjust. Also it would be wrong to imagine that coming to terms with loss is an all or nothing affair. Each person's history, and therefore each person's loss, is different. Each person will mourn in their own way. However, the idea of complicated mourning is an important one. Delayed, disguised, prolonged and exaggerated grief reactions all indicate that the process of mourning has been seriously interrupted in such a way that the person is not moving towards rebuilding their life. The bereaved person seems to be hindered from moving towards the fourth Phase of Mourning, that of 'Reorganisation', or the fourth Task, that of relocating the deceased and moving on with life.

This information on 'complicated mourning' is presented as a general guide only, as indicating the type of response to loss that may require professional help. The material should be sufficient to allow a concerned relative, friend or neighbour to suggest, diplomatically, to the bereaved person that they may benefit from talking to someone with training in the field of bereavement, or to discuss these concerns with a GP, or one of the organisations described below.

Who is at risk?

As noted above some researchers suggest as many as one third of all those experiencing a major loss will experience some form of complicated mourning, the most common being prolonged grief. A number of risk factors, which make complications more likely to occur, have been identified. We will consider some of the more important factors under three headings: 'Types of death'; 'Characteristics of the relationship and of the mourner' (these two areas will be treated together as they are in practice very difficult to separate); and 'Social circumstances'.

Types of death

Deaths that have occurred unexpectedly, suddenly, and perhaps violently, are often particularly difficult to mourn. These would include deaths from accidents, suicide or murder. Losing someone through suicide is undoubtedly one of the most disturbing losses that can be experienced. In addition to the grief provoked by the loss, someone who has been bereaved through suicide will have to struggle with the enormously painful question: 'Whose fault was it?' If the person who has killed themself is regarded as responsible for their own death, then the bereaved person will naturally feel that the suicide, to some extent at least, was a rejection of them, and a dismissal of their grief: 'If she had loved us she wouldn't have done it'. Such thoughts will be associated with intense hurt, and what is often particularly difficult to accept, deep anger. In many cases people close to someone who has committed suicide blame themselves, for not responding to early warnings, or not helping enough, or not realising how desperate the person was. This view will often lead to profound feelings of guilt. All this must often be dealt with in the context of the profound social stigma attached to suicide. In addition to the pain of loss, suicide may leave the bereaved person feeling rejected, angry, guilty, or ashamed. Many of those suffering loss through suicide will experience all of these feelings as they struggle to make sense of what has happened. This seems to be true regardless of when the suicide has occurred, but there are additional difficulties for children who lose a parent or other close family member through suicide. One is that they may not be told. The response of other family members may suggest feelings of guilt or embarrassment and the child may come to feel that whatever happened is too dreadful to speak about. Another complicating factor is where the suicide occurs in the home and the child is aware of what has happened, perhaps discovering the body or even witnessing the suicide. Such situations greatly exacerbate the experience of loss, and some researchers would argue that the risk of some form of complicated mourning developing is so high that any child in this situation should receive some professional help with their grief.

In recent years a lot of attention has been given to the impact of loss when the death has occurred suddenly in accidents which have resulted in large-scale loss of life. Accidents involving coaches, aircraft, ships, crowds at football stadiums, fires, and similar traumatic circumstances, may leave the bereaved person facing multiple losses. Preoccupation with the circumstances of the loss, perhaps experiencing hallucinations of the accident, and suffering various aspects of grief in a severe form, are common features of such traumatic losses.

For some people the response to the trauma of their loss has particular characteristics that make the condition significantly different from that of exaggerated grief reaction described above. The term 'Post-Traumatic Stress Disorder' refers to a particular cluster of signs and symptoms that requires specialised help that is significantly different from the forms of complicated mourning described in this chapter. ·

Characteristics of the relationship and of the mourner
There are particular types of loss that more commonly lead to complications. Loss of a partner, or child, or losing a parent when under fifteen, are particularly difficult losses to come to terms with. But more important than these general types of loss is the nature of the relationship that is severed by the loss. If the relationship involved high levels of dependence, or if the relationship contained very mixed feelings (in particular strong but contradictory feelings of affection and anger), complications in mourning may develop.

It seems that there may be certain personality types that are more prone to grief than others. Personal characteristics such as a tendency to cling to others, to pine when separated; a tendency towards feelings of insecurity, anxiety, low self-esteem, excessive anger or self-criticism; and previous experience of major psychological problems can make a person vulnerable to complicated mourning. Previous history of loss is also significant, especially if the mourning from a previous loss has not been completed. An inability to express feelings is also a risk factor that is often a major difficulty for men who have suffered a significant loss.

It is also clear that responses to loss are influenced by the sort of attachments that have been formed. In chapter 1 we noted that children can form different types of attachments. We noted four basic types: one 'secure' and three 'insecure'; the insecure types have been called 'resistant', 'avoidant' and 'disorganised'. The type of attachment appears to determine the response an infant will have to separation. Research has shown that in adult life also attachments of different types are formed. Some people tend to form insecure attachments that are characterised by anxiety, dependency, clinging, and perhaps anger. Others tend to form insecure attachments characterised by a lack of emotion, independence and detachment. Whereas a tendency to form secure attachments contributes to uncomplicated mourning, it appears that a tendency to form insecure attachments contributes to experiencing complications in mourning. Broadly speaking, a tendency to form insecure attachments of the anxious, clinging type appears to predispose a person to develop prolonged or exaggerated grief reactions, whereas a tendency to form insecure attachments involving self-protective detachment predisposes to delayed or disguised grief reactions.

Social circumstances

We have noted in chapter 7 that where a bereaved person feels helped and supported by others, adapting to loss is facilitated. But complications in the process of mourning are more likely to develop where the bereaved person feels unsupported, or perhaps insufficiently supported by family, friends and neighbours. There may be many reasons why such help does not seem to be forthcoming: perhaps there really are no social supports available, or perhaps help has not been of an appropriate kind, or offered in a clear way, or perhaps the bereaved person is simply unable to recognise what is available or what is being offered. But the key question is whether the mourner *feels* supported. In addition to help from family, friends or neighbours – or perhaps in the absence of such help – many bereaved people find support through religious or cultural associations. Again the likelihood of developing complications in mourning can be increased where such associations have been disrupted for some reason, for example through moving home. Other factors that can make bereavement more difficult to bear include being unemployed or in a job that is disliked. There are additional stresses that make it more likely that the mourner will isolate themselves. In the short term, having dependent children at home can be an additional stress that may complicate mourning, but it seems in the long run that having a dependent family can be helpful as it encourages the mourner to adjust and attend to the requirements of moving on with life.

Counselling and therapy

Most people will come to terms with their loss without assist-ance from counsellors or therapists. Most help, both practical and emotional, comes through family, friends and neighbours. Often what we might describe as informal support from a GP or nurse has also helped with the process of mourning. None of this would be regarded as counselling or therapy in the formal sense, but these contacts provide valuable opportunities to share feelings and can be very helpful to the bereaved person. However, there has been an increase in awareness of the needs of bereaved people in recent years and counselling and therapy services are available both within and outside the National Health Service.

Sources within the National Health Service

Some workers in this field suggest that everyone who has experienced a major bereavement can benefit from some con-tact with a counsellor or therapist, if only for one or a few appointments. It is further suggested that there should be a large-scale expansion of services so that some form of counsel-ling or therapy is available for all bereaved people who would like to take advantage of the provision. In terms of such large-scale provision being made by the National Health Service there have been three main arguments against the suggestion. Firstly, as has been noted, most people adapt to their loss without requiring bereavement counselling or therapy. Secondly, research indicates that many bereaved people would consider the attentions of a counsellor or therapist intrusive. And thirdly, there is the question of cost. Given the scarcity of resources, it is argued, help should be restricted to those who really need it, those who are not able to mourn effectively, that is those who are experiencing some form of complicated mourning.

Although in some situations counselling may be offered to all bereaved families – for example when a death has occurred in a hospice – it is very unlikely that this will be available on a large scale. In practice counselling or therapy is likely to be offered only to the minority who experience complications. Within the broad description of complicated mourning there will be a range from relatively minor to major disruptions of the mourning process. All such difficulties can benefit from specialist help.

But in addition to those clearly experiencing some form of complicated mourning many would argue that provision should be made to offer preventive help to those who are clearly 'at risk' of developing complications. This means identifying those with the sort of risk factors outlined in the previous section of this chapter and offering them help early on. Although this may happen in some areas it really depends on what help is available locally and the level of awareness of GPs and other potential referrers.

There are many kinds of counselling and therapy available but the overall goal of most approaches is to identify how the process of mourning is being distorted or obstructed and to help the mourner complete the process effectively. In terms of the Four Tasks of Mourning this means helping the bereaved person accept the loss has occurred, experience and express the feelings associated with the loss, adjust to the loss 'internally', and rebuild their life without the deceased. Just as there are many types of complication there are various methods of helping. Often counselling and therapy are distinguished in terms of the severity of the problem addressed. Counsellors, it is claimed, are equipped to help with relatively minor complications while therapists are trained to work with more difficult problems. However, I think it is a mistake to take this distinction too seriously. Just because someone has many years of formal training and experience in general counselling or therapy it does not follow that they are well equipped to work with complicated mourning. A counsellor who has specialised in bereavement may have comparatively less formal training but may be much more able to help than someone with extensive general training in therapy but little experience in bereavement work. If a counsellor or therapist is consulted it is advisable to ask about qualifications and experience in this type of work. Whoever works in this field will not only need formal training, they will also need to have worked with their own grief, and their own anxieties about death.

Referral to a National Health Service counsellor or therapist is usually made through a GP. The counsellor or therapist may be based in a hospital or at a GP's surgery, or they may work in the community visiting people in their homes. A common pattern is for the bereaved person to be seen once or twice a week initially, reducing gradually to once a month or every six weeks.

This will take several months and may involve being seen for up to twenty sessions, depending on the severity of the difficulties. Most people can be significantly helped with half this number of appointments, but some will need more.

Services outside the National Health Service

Outside the National Health Service there are a number of organisations offering counselling to people who have suffered bereavements. In particular it is worth noting the work of CRUSE. This organisation has contacts throughout Britain and can offer guidance on all aspects of bereavement. Their counsellors are specially trained to work with bereavement. This help can be provided directly, by letter or by phone, and at different locations including the bereaved person's home. Information can be obtained from the headquarters of CRUSE. (Addresses and telephone numbers of the organisations mentioned in this chapter are provided in Appendix 1 at the end of this book.) Local branches of CRUSE can be found in telephone directories. The National Association of Bereavement Services has compiled an extensive dictionary of various bereavement services available in Britain, and information on counsellors, therapists and organisations can be obtained through the British Association for Counselling. There are many organisations focusing on particular types of loss: some of these are listed in Appendix 1.

Befriending

Most people who suffer a major loss will not develop the sort of complications outlined earlier in this chapter. Given the scarcity of resources it is likely that formal counselling or therapy will be available only for those who do experience difficulties such as delayed, disguised, prolonged, or exaggerated grief. Although some people who may be at risk of developing some form of complicated grief may have the opportunity of receiving counselling or therapy as a way of preventing such complications, this is likely to remain very much a local provision. But while counselling and therapy are likely to be restricted to a minority of those suffering bereavements, another source of support is potentially appropriate to all who suffer loss. 'Befriending' refers to any act of help, encouragement or support given to one in need. In the general sense anyone – relative, friend, or neighbour – who responds with concern to someone in mourning is 'befriending' them. But there are a number of organisations in Britain that have established 'befriending' networks, which enable contacts to be made between someone who has suffered a loss, and those willing to respond through sharing and support. Help is offered by volunteers, and is of a very informal kind. A befriender is not a trained counsellor or therapist. In many cases a befriender is someone who has experienced a major loss themselves and has subsequently offered to make contact with others who have been bereaved in order to offer support. One organisation, The Compassionate Friends, generally tries to offer recently bereaved people contact with someone who has themselves been bereaved for at least two years. The Ananda Network also has a network of volunteer befrienders offering contact and support to those who have been bereaved or those facing their own death. This network is associated with The Buddhist Hospice Trust which aims to bring together 'the teachings of the Buddha and the philosophy of modern hospice care'. Their befriending service, operating through The Ananda Network, offers support regardless of religious affiliation, or lack of it. CRUSE, whose counselling service was mentioned in the previous section, also coordinates an extensive network of informal support and help for the bereaved. Enquiries can be made to the headquarters of CRUSE or to one of their local branches which may be found in the local telephone directory.

Summary

Although most people suffering bereavements are helped through support from family, friends and neighbours, other sources of help are available. For those experiencing some form of complicated mourning, help from a trained counsellor or therapist is advisable. This help can be obtained through a GP referral, or through one of the organisations listed in Appendix 1. While those requiring counselling or therapy are likely to be a minority of those suffering bereavement, many more could benefit from receiving support through one of the informal 'befriending' networks.

9 Facing the future

A general principle of all growth and development is that change occurs in discontinuous steps. The process of growth occurs through alternating periods of temporary disintegration followed by reintegration at a different level. Another way of expressing this point would be to say that development occurs through a process of rebuilding, or reconstructing, a new form after an old one has been dismantled. This principle can be clearly observed in the way children develop motor skills, and in the way they develop psychologically. In order for a new skill to develop the child necessarily passes through a period of clumsiness and uncertainty before the new pattern is established. A child's physical and psychological growth occurs discontinuously, or in other words, in 'spurts'.

Recovering from the loss of a loved one also requires personal growth. Death challenges us to grow psychologically and spiritually (using the word in its broadest sense). The process of mourning is clearly characterised by the same general principle which underlies all growth and development. Earlier patterns of behaviour, thought and feeling disintegrate, and new patterns must be developed to replace the old. This temporary breakdown of old patterns can feel like the destruction of everything that has been of value in a person's life. But in the process of mourning construction follows destruction: a new structure emerges to replace the old. This general principle is reflected in Bowlby's description of the Four Phases of Mourning. Self-protective 'Numbness' is followed by a period of 'Disorganisation' that can involve angry protest, despair, withdrawal and depression. The mourner may feel they are 'falling apart', or 'going to pieces'. This sense of disintegration forms the early stages of a process aimed at reconstruction or reintegration, or as Bowlby terms it 'Reorganisation'. What feels like destruction is followed by reconstruction; but it can be very difficult to believe this when everything seems to be collapsing into chaos.

Carol was the only survivor of a road traffic accident in which her mother, her husband and her two-year-old son (her only child) died. The accident occurred when they were returning from a holiday. Carol was driving and she recalled being very angry with her husband because he had insisted they return home earlier than they had planned because he wanted to complete some work that he had left unfinished. After the accident Carol was in turmoil. How does someone adjust to such a loss? As a result of that single event Carol had ceased to be a mother and had ceased to be a wife; she was also now without any living parent. So much of Carol's life had been disrupted, so much destroyed. From such devastation and destruction it may seem to be impossible to rebuild. But somehow Carol did manage to recover and reconstruct her life. She described her struggle as follows:

> At first there just seemed to be no point in continuing. I just could not understand why I was alive. The accident was my fault, but I was the only one to survive. It all seemed so wrong. I mean my life, everything that was important to me, had gone, and I had destroyed it, so why was I still here? I couldn't talk to anyone or do anything, I just wanted to die. Over time the months and months of longing gave way to more of a sadness. Gradually my feelings changed. It started to feel as if Dan, George and Mum were with me. I knew, of course, that they had gone, but I felt them sort of inside but real, not just imagination. After a while it seemed as if they were helping me, encouraging me to take care of myself, go out and do things and meet people, and most of all to stop blaming myself. It took a long time but eventually I felt as if life was worth living again – not that I don't miss them, or love them any less, but it felt like I was doing what they would want me to do, almost like I had their blessing to enjoy life again.

Carol describes the process of 'Disorganisation' followed by 'Reorganisation'. We may note that her description illustrates Worden's Four Tasks of Mourning very well. In particular, what Worden calls 'relocating' the deceased is vividly described. She was able to let go of them as people 'out there' and relocate them 'inside'. Carol also expressed her appreciation of a small number of close friends who were unobtrusively available, even when she kept rejecting their offers of help.

> At first I couldn't bear to see anyone or talk to anyone. I know I gave some of my friends a very hard time. But a few somehow let me

know they were with me, they were there if I needed them. It took a long time before I could respond but eventually I did spend time with them, and gradually the loneliness started to lift. I began to feel a strong connection to the friends who were still there, still available. They didn't act in a superior way, or pity me. It was a feeling of support that was somehow much more mutual – the best word I guess is that I felt a sense of solidarity with them. That helped a lot.

There is a story in the Buddhist tradition about a mother, Krishna Gotami, who after having lost her husband two years before, was bereaved of her young son. She had experienced many difficulties in her life, including poverty and loss, but the death of her young son threatened to overwhelm her. Racked with grief, Krishna Gotami carried her dead child in her arms through her village calling out of help, pleading that someone do something to bring her son back to life. She was inconsolable. Eventually, in the evening, the village elder suggested she find the Buddha and ask for his help. Krishna Gotami left the village and walked all night to the place where she was told the Buddha was staying. In the early morning she found the Buddha and approached him. With her dead child still in her arms, she begged for his help. The Buddha saw her grief and said he would help, but she must fetch him a handful of mustard seed. 'But', said the Buddha, 'the mustard seed must come from a house that has not known death, a house in which no-one has died'. Krishna Gotami hurried back to her village, still carrying her son's body, to ask her friends for the mustard seed. At the first house she asked for the mustard seed and was immediately given what she requested. However, when she asked, 'Has there been a death in this household?', the reply came back, 'Alas, the living are few, but the dead are many. Do not remind us of our deepest grief'. While there were many households who would readily give her what she asked she could find none that had not suffered loss. Eventually, after visiting every house, she fell by the wayside, exhausted. It was evening and, still carrying her dead son, she walked through the night back to the Buddha. In the early morning she approached the Buddha, saying: 'I have understood the teaching of the Compassionate One. I am not alone in my grief'. She then lay the body of her son on the ground before the Buddha.

There are many things we can learn from this story; the part I would like to emphasise is that it highlights that being alone in one's grief is a burden that can only be put down through experiencing some form of connection with others – some form of 'solidarity', as Carol expressed it. When Krishna Gotami saw that she was not alone in her grief she was able to lay down her burden, her dead son, and the terrible pain of yearning that he be brought back to life. She lay the body of her dead son at the feet of the Buddha. Perhaps a Christian would express this as offering one's suffering to God, or unburdening one's suffering before God. A sense of connection with others, knowing we are not alone in our grief, helps us to let go, put down our burden of pain and sorrow, and move on with life. Carol found that laying down her burden of grief involved letting go of blame and self-criticism, letting go of 'If only…', letting go of trying to turn back the clock. For Carol, as for many others, this process of moving on with life was intricately bound up with her relationships, both long-standing friendships and those newly formed:

> I knew I just had to move forward and reach out to life despite the pain. At first it seemed impossible, but I just kept going, making the effort to see people and spend time with them. In the end that's what got me through. I started to enjoy being with friends, and my life started to make sense again.

Appendix 1
Some useful addresses

AGE CONCERN
Astral House, 1268 London Road, London, SW16 4ER. (Tel: 0181 679 8000)

THE ANANDA NETWORK/THE BUDDHIST HOSPICE TRUST
PO Box 123, Ashford, Kent, TN24 9TF. (Tel: c/o Ray Wills 0181 789 6170)

ASSOCIATION FOR DEATH EDUCATION AND COUNSELLING
638, Prospect Avenue, Hertford, CT 06105-4298, USA.

BRITISH ASSOCIATION FOR COUNSELLING
1 Regent Place, Rugby, Warwickshire, CV21 2PJ. (Tel: 01788 578328; office 550899)

THE BRITISH HUMANIST ASSOCIATION
14 Lambs Conduit Passage, London, WC1R 4AH. (Tel: 0171 430 0908)

CANCERLINK
17 Britannia Street, London, WC1X 9JN. (Tel: 0171 833 2451)

CANCER RELIEF MACMILLAN FUND
Anchor House, 15-19 Britten Street, London, SW3 3TZ. (Tel: 0171 351 7811)

CARERS' NATIONAL ASSOCIATION
29 Chilworth Mews, London, W2 3RG. (Tel: 0171 724 7776)

CENTRE FOR LIVING WITH LOSS
Charlottesville, Virginia, USA.

THE COT DEATH SOCIETY
116 Alt Road, Formby, Merseyside, L37 8BW. (Tel: 017048 70005)

THE COMPASSIONATE FRIENDS
53 North Street, Bristol, BS3 1EN. (Tel: 01179 539 639)

CRUSE BEREAVEMENT CARE
Cruse House, 126 Sheen Road, Richmond, Surrey, TW9 1UR. (Tel: 0181 940 4818), and local branches

ELIZABETH KÜBLER-ROSS CENTRE
Headwaters, Virginia 2442, USA.

THE HOSPICE INFORMATION SERVICE
St. Christopher's Hospice, 51-59 Lawrie Park Road, Sydenham, London, SE26 6DZ. (Tel: 0181 778 9252)

LESBIAN AND GAY BEREAVEMENT PROJECT
Vaughan M. Williams Centre, Colindale Hospital, London, NW9 5GJ. (Tel: helpline 0181 455 8894: admin. 0181 200 0511)

MARIE CURIE CANCER CARE
28 Belgrave Square, London, SW1X 8QG. (Tel: 0171 235 3325)

NATIONAL ASSOCIATION OF BEREAVEMENT SERVICES
20 Norton Folgate, London, E1 6DB. (Tel: referrals 0171 247 1080; admin. 0171 247 0617)

NATIONAL SECRETARY
NATIONAL ASSOCIATION OF FUNERAL DIRECTORS
618 Warwick Road, Solihull, West Midlands, B91 1AA. (Tel: 0121 711 1343)

NATIONAL ASSOCIATION OF WIDOWS
54-57 Allison Street, Digbeth, Birmingham, B5 5TH. (Tel: 0121 643 8348)

NATIONAL BLACK BEREAVEMENT FOUNDATION
25 Baysham Street, Camden, London, NW1. (Tel: 0171 388 5551)

THE NATURAL DEATH CENTRE
20 Heber Road, London NW2 6AA. (Tel: 0181 208 2853)

PROBATE REGISTRY
Personal Applications Dept., Second Floor, Principal Registry, Family Division, Somerset House, Strand, London, WC2R 1LP. (Tel: 0171 936 6983 or 6974)

THE STILLBIRTH AND NEONATAL DEATH SOCIETY (SANDS)
28 Portland Place, London, W1N 4DE. (Tel: 0171 436 5881)

TERENCE HIGGINS TRUST
(a registered charity to inform, advise and help on AIDS and HIV infection)
52-54 Grays Inn Road, London, WC1X 8JU. (Tel: admin 0171 831 0330; helpline 12 noon to 10pm daily 0171 242 1010)

THE WILL REGISTRY
357-361 Lewisham High Street, London, SE13 6NZ.

Appendix 2
Suggestions for further reading

The Natural Death Handbook, Nicholas Albery, Gil Elliot and Joseph Elliot (eds) (Virgin Books, London, 1993)
The Hour of our Death, Philippe Ariès (Penguin, London, 1981)
Loss, John Bowlby (Penguin, London, 1980)
I Don't Know What to Say - How to Help and Support Someone Who is Dying, Robert Buckman (Macmillan Papermac, London, 1990)
Death, Dying and Bereavement, Donna Dickenson and Malcolm Johnson (Sage, London, 1990)
The Limits of Medicine, Ivan Illich (Pelican, London, 1977)
On Death and Dying, Elizabeth Kübler-Ross (Tavistock Publications, 1969)
Death: The Final Stage of Growth, Elizabeth Kübler-Ross (ed.) (Prentice Hall, 1975)
Who Dies? Stephen Levine (Gateway Books, Bath, 1986)
A Grief Observed, C. S. Lewis (Faber & Faber, London, 1966)
How We Die, Sherwin B. Nuland (Chatto and Windus, London, 1994)
Bereavement, Colin Murray Parkes (Penguin, London, 1985)
The Anatomy of Bereavement, Beverley Raphael, (Routledge, London, 1984)
Acquainted with the Night - a Year on the Frontier of Death, Allegra Taylor (Fontana, London, 1989)
Wills and Probate, Which? Books (Consumers' Assocation, London, 1988)
Grief Counselling and Grief Therapy, J. William Worden, (Routledge, London 1991, 2nd ed)
Funerals Without God: A Practical Guide to Non-religious Funerals, Jane Wynne Willson (British Humanist Assocation, London, 1989)